THE
CAN-DO
MANAGER

THE
CAN-DO
MANAGER

HOW TO GET
YOUR EMPLOYEES
TO TAKE RISKS,
TAKE ACTION,
AND GET
THINGS DONE

TESS KIRBY

amacom
AMERICAN MANAGEMENT ASSOCIATION

Library of Congress Cataloging-in-Publication Data

Kirby, Tess, 1943–
    The can-do manager : how to get your employees to take risks, take action, and
    get things done / Tess Kirby.
        p.   cm.
    Includes index.
    ISBN 0-8144-5887-4
    1. Employee motivation.   2. Executive ability.   3. Success in
    business.   I. Title.
    HF5549.5.M63K57   1989
    658.3'14—dc20   89-45453
                                                                           CIP

Printing number

10

*With admiration, love, and respect
for my sons,
who have taught me so much*

Contents

Preface

It's no longer news that the business of being a manager is changing. Instead of operating in a safe environment run by tried-and-true methods, these days you're asked to chart unknown, tricky, and sometimes treacherous waters. To be a success in this new world of business, you must change your role from that of controller and director to one of coach, teacher, leader, and cheerleader. You are required to do more with less, so you need to bring out the best in your employees, squeezing the greatest motivation and productivity from them in spite of fewer resources.

I wrote this book to help the managers who have asked how to best make this transition. I surveyed the existing books and tapes, but had trouble finding one source that gave practical pointers to managers on the front lines. Several books tell wonderful, inspirational stories of businesses with loyal, excited employees who go not only the extra mile but an extra ten miles without being asked. These employees show creativity and responsibility while taking some very smart risks for their companies. But most of these books spotlight the CEO or founder of the company, and they describe the top-level practices that make their organizations so action-oriented and successful.

After reading these success stories, the nuts-and-bolts manager asks, "What can I do? I don't run the company. I just run my division or department." I offer this book as a practical answer to that question. Though only one of many managers in a company, you can make a difference. This book deals with the situations you face daily: hiring, training, dealing with mistakes and conflicts, making decisions, and motivating your staff to be the best it can be. I offer this book as a practical, how-to-pull-it-off guide. It deals with what you *can* accomplish when you aren't the president of the company and have to work within a limited sphere.

The methods I have presented here have been successful for the thousands of managers with whom I have had the privilege to work during the past few years. I am grateful to those who shared their stories of accomplishment, and many of their experiences are described in this book. By using proven methods, these managers have transformed individuals assigned to the same department or work group into smoothly functioning, highly productive, self-confident teams. Likewise, these managers have reshaped the members of such teams into stimulating, exciting, and motivated workers with a reborn loyalty in spite of uncertain times.

My hope is that this book will help you on the journey to a different way of doing business. The focus here is on what you—the nuts-and-bolts manager—can do to capitalize on this new world of work.

Chapter 1

Create a Turned-on Team

For a business to survive—let alone thrive—in today's world, everyone in the company must have an action orientation, from the housekeeper right on up to the president. Many managers are good risk-takers themselves. Often, that is the reason they have risen to the positions they have. Yet although they themselves are intelligent risk-takers, they don't really know how to turn their employees into action-oriented players. Even the most cautious member of a team can become a turned-on worker ready for action. In this chapter, we'll focus on ways to create a can-do team that duplicates some of a manager's skill at taking risks.

WHO ARE THE ACTION-ORIENTED PEOPLE?

The kinds of actions that make a company successful aren't necessarily the huge, highly publicized, do-or-die risks. They are day-to-day chances such as trying a new way to process paperwork, experimenting with a new marketing technique, or solving a problem in an innovative way. The atmosphere is one of action and movement. There's an attitude of doing something about a situation instead of complaining or suffering in silence. What type of person takes these chances? People who move into action demonstrate several characteristics that differentiate them from people who prefer the tried-and-true, from those who wait for instructions and then complain when they get them.

People who get excited about going to work have a sense of self-confidence. They are individuals who go the extra mile: they solve the existing problems and look for new problems to solve because they believe they'll be successful. They're fun to be around, and others enjoy working with them because they chalk up successes. An air of enthusiasm surrounds risk-takers, and it is catching. They have experienced success along the way, and they draw on that success to create more success. Action-oriented people have a feeling of control. They don't depend on luck to bring themselves good fortune; they create their own luck and their own opportunities. They have faith that when mistakes happen—as they inevitably must when exploring the new and different—they can parlay them into something useful instead of being crippled by them.

People who get things done set goals that mean something to them. Men and women in the new work force no longer want simply to pay the mortgage, treat themselves to a nice vacation, or be able to afford college for the kids. Both experienced and inexperienced workers now want to be able to provide these necessities and luxuries by doing work that is meaningful for them. They view themselves as making a contribution to a larger picture. Can-do people know the score for their actions. They know when they are on target; and when they're not, they take steps to remedy that situation.

People who are action oriented are optimistic about the results of their actions, and they believe that something good will come from those actions. Having the necessary skills to take intelligent chances, they select risks that are well thought out, and they give themselves the best chance for success. They know how to set goals that will motivate them, and how to plan so that those goals get accomplished. They know how to make decisions that can be supported and that will accomplish their goals. People who are action oriented feel a sense of power. They believe they have the opportunity for autonomy, self-expression, and personal commitment.

WHERE DO YOU FIND THESE PEOPLE?

At this point you may be sighing, "Great, but where do I find a staff with all these qualities?" You don't. You create one. The skills and techniques to accomplish this aren't difficult to master or particularly mysterious. To create the action team, your most important ingredient is a willingness to take the risk yourself. By your efforts and with the suggestions in this book, you can mold a team that displays these characteristics.

Your present work force may consist of people who fall short of being on the job 100 percent of the time, mentally or physically. Some recent studies have shown that less than 25 percent of American workers say they perform at their full potential. Fifty percent have said that they put no more into their jobs than they have to to keep them. Seventy-five percent have reported that they could be a lot more effective than they are, and 60 percent have reported that they don't work as hard as they used to.

You, as manager, have the power to turn this around, but it requires a sharing of power. You no longer can be the focus of attention and control. Instead of being the director and controller, you have to be a coach, clearing the path for your team to do its job and getting out of its way when the staff starts rolling by. It means focusing on goals and putting in place a plan to reach those goals. It requires garnering the necessary resources and keeping the wolf from the door, as well as making room for taking risks and bragging about your staff's accomplishments.

WHAT IS YOUR NEW ROLE?

The manager's job is to let the action-oriented people know when they are performing well and help them get back on track when they aren't. You need to listen to their ideas and use them. You must support their risk taking by encouraging them to try new methods and work on new ideas. You also need the ability to teach your staff skills that people usually don't pick up along the way—skills that are necessary for succeeding at this risk-taking business. There are ways to solve problems, set goals, or plan and make decisions that encourage a can-do attitude. You can teach these skills, which are the tools for intelligent risk taking. When you do all this, your employees will make and carry out decisions you can support. You will create a work force that can adapt to the nonroutine, that can deal with unpredictable situations that pop up daily.

Not only is taking risks the new management mandate and the very heart of a new approach to managing, but it's always been good business. When staff members feel free—even encouraged—to take chances and are given the resources to do so in the form of advice, money, time, and tools, they are more committed to their jobs. They own a piece of the action, if not physically at least psychologically, and they are willing to do more to further their ideas. They are committed to their jobs, which is what promotes going that extra mile, investing that extra time and energy. Their payoff is a feeling of success and confidence. Motivation, commitment, and energy increase when people have the skills to be successful. Having a committed, motivated, and energized staff is invaluable in meeting today's demands for increased productivity.

HOW DO YOU ACHIEVE THESE GOALS?

Perhaps you can name people on your staff whom you believe would never become action oriented, no matter how many resources you threw at them and how much encouragement you gave them. Possibly, they've never had the chance to find out how exciting it can be to get their ideas off the ground. They may never have experienced being part of the decision-making process and may never have had their ideas listened to, let alone implemented.

Remember that you haven't hired "new" people; you've always hired "used" people. These "used" people have come to you with a history of working for other managers and have had other work experiences. Perhaps their opinions were never asked. Possibly, in past jobs they came up with innovative ideas, just to have them shot down because their supervisors didn't believe it was a worker's job to make suggestions. Maybe they learned resentment at another job, and their enthusiasm was turned off. It's amazing what talents come forth when people are given some encouragement, some information and coaching, regarding sensible goal setting, planning, decision making, and risk taking. Managers who have coached and worked with such "used" individuals have been astounded at how some stars start to shine when they never would have expected a glimmer from behind the clouds.

A turned-on work group is there 100 percent of the time—both physically and mentally. The need to go somewhere else to feel in control or successful or to make an important contribution is gone. The employees realize they can receive these rewards at work as well as elsewhere. The urge to leave at 5:00 P.M. or to just slide through the day weakens or even dies.

You derive many benefits from creating a can-do, turned-on team. Your management sees you as an accomplished leader who does a quality job. Other managers wonder what magic you've wrought to reduce complaints and absenteeism as well as increase productivity. They are envious, watching employees line up to work in your section.

MY COMPANY DOESN'T WORK
THIS WAY

Some companies are still blind to the need for an innovative, creative work force. They refuse to acknowledge that creativity should be encouraged, drawn from all individuals in the company and not just from the higher ranks. If you work for a company that still has this philosophy, it remains in your best interests to hone the skills you need to create a turned-on team. What a company is blind to today may turn into its mandate tomorrow. The wave of the future is empowerment of employees and maximization of their skills.

Stanley was an engineer for one of the automobile companies. Cradle-to-grave security was imbedded in that industry's culture, and security was one of the main reasons he joined the firm twenty years earlier. Life at the company became even more appealing when the thirty-and-out policy was introduced. Stan had ten years until he could retire, which was exactly what he planned to do. He was the first to tell anyone what a terrific job he had: it provided a good salary, not too much pressure, and enjoyable work on the whole. He didn't have to deal with a lot of change or risk. He counted on that situation to stay pretty stable for the rest of his working life.

Stanley's life turned upside down in the space of three months. Management realized that it needed to change a number of its practices if the company was to survive. In an effort to turn the huge enterprise around, management declared massive white-collar layoffs. There were calls for a different type of behavior from the remaining staff. Risk taking, which had been discouraged before, was to become the rule, not the exception. Stanley was put in charge of his activity, which was being turned into a profit center; black ink was expected by the end of one year. Stan believed that if he didn't meet that goal, he would be out on the street. Quite a switch.

Since the only guarantee anyone works with anymore is that change is always around the corner, the smart money has people preparing themselves. Recent research shows that the entrepreneurial spirit and intelligent risk taking is the only way to survive, let alone be successful. Companies that don't foster innovation on the part of all workers are going to die. So you will need to have the skills to create an action team, whether your company is going to pull an about-face and change all the rules or you have to search for employment elsewhere because the company fails. Sharpen your skills now because you'll need them eventually.

STEPS TO A TURNED-ON TEAM

You can learn how to choose people for your team who already have some of these qualities in place. There are ways to build a staff that will work together and feel like a team from the start. These are not complicated techniques; they are just some things that you may not have thought of yet. The top motivator for workers is achievement at their jobs. You are critical in making that happen. The way you select, train, and orient your staff has a big impact on its success rate. Chapters 2 and 3 that follow provide a framework for accomplishing this task.

How you react to your employees' attempts at action will have a lot to do with how turned on they remain. If you greet their mistakes and first tries with discouragement or expect perfection of them, their action orientation will be squelched in no time. Instead, teach your staff to parlay these mistakes into successes through problem solving (discussed in Chapter 5). Chapter 4 will help you avoid the common managerial mistakes that inhibit an action attitude.

Lots of times, people are ready not only to adjust to change but to initiate it (see Chapter 6). Often, however, they interfere with their own good intentions. There are things a manager can do to ensure these people don't trip as they move toward success. Chapter 7 explains how to open the door to an action attitude. Taking risks can be a scary proposition, but Chapter 8 describes steps you can take to reduce the downside of that action. Give a benevolent, gentle push to assist your employees into making the plunge (as described in Chapter 13).

Certain skills are necessary for people to take intelligent risks and have them be successful. You can guide your staff in setting sensible goals—not only short-term goals but long-term ones as well. Also, goals that link people's personal desires with the company's needs guarantee highest productivity. Chapter 10 offers a simple planning model that ensures such goals get accomplished in a quality way.

Action and control often boil down to decent decision making. This is one of the pieces of authority you share with employees as you build their power. Chapter 12 gives a simple decision model that can be used in ten minutes, ensuring that the decisions your employees make when you're not around will be ones you can support and be proud of. Conflict is a natural part of decision making and action. Chapter 9 discusses conflict-resolving skills, which are critical to your success.

This book features practical, simple steps you can take today to create an enthusiastic, can-do team distinguished by its quality work and terrific attitude. You have the power to create the team that takes risks, takes action, and gets things done.

Chapter 2

Building an Action
Attitude From the Start

Whether your employees have the can-do attitude that climbs over obstacles, initiates change, and follows through on jobs depends on the climate you set. One of the ways you create this climate is by the practices you choose in hiring, orienting, and training your employees.

If you make an effort to select your team from people who show an action attitude, you send a message to both the new people and the ones who are already in place: action is something you value and expect. If you carefully orient the new people to the team, so that they feel competent and already like insiders, you punch that message home. Your attention to training lets them know in yet another way just what you want their contribution to be. By selecting, orienting, and training new people with an eye toward creating a group of individuals with confidence and capabilities, you'll reap the benefits of a group of employees who will do the jobs you want according to your standards, with a positive and enthusiastic spirit. They will be proud of their work and their membership on your team. An added benefit is that other employees, who aren't on the team and who have these same traits, will want to become part of the group, too. Because of this, you'll always have a pool of talented, eager people waiting for an opening.

CHOOSE "CAN-DO" PEOPLE FOR YOUR TEAM

The interviewing process makes many managers and supervisors quite nervous, and reasonably so. Decisions they make about whom they hire will have to be lived with for a long time. Also, other people will make judgments about their abilities based on these hiring decisions. People in a position to hire are often intimidated by the process itself. They're afraid they won't be able keep the interview going well or that they will lose control. They dread those deadly silences that in reality are often only thirty seconds long, even though they seem to drag on into the next century.

The usual pattern for an interview is you as interviewer set a comfortable climate by offering the candidate a cup of coffee and having a little chit-chat about the weather, the parking, or current events. Next, you offer information about the job and the expectations. You may take the person on a tour of the work site and give the candidate an opportunity to ask questions. The next step is to ask some questions to determine how well the potential employee matches the needs of the job. You both then shake hands and say good-bye.

After interviewing the two, three, or four persons who are most likely, you call their former employers to get some recommendations. These comments are usually glowing because everyone is afraid of lawsuits these days. You then try to remember your impressions of the candidate and sort through the notes of the meeting. Then you make a decision and hope it's the right one. Unfortunately, research shows that the decision is usually based on an opinion formed about the candidate during the first thirty seconds of the interview. Comments to justify the choice are, "They acted like the kind of person who takes action," or, "They seemed as if they would fit in okay."

Instead of relying on this standard interviewing strategy to make some pretty heavy decisions, try the following method to give you confidence in the process and make it more productive. It's a way to keep the interview moving with you in control. Best of all, this method assures that you make the best choice among the candidates you have.

Restructure the Interview

Instead of structuring the interview so that, after the chit-chat, you share information about the job, ask a few questions, and maybe give a tour, arrange the format a bit differently. After the chit-chat, ask the candidates questions about themselves, then share information about the job and take a tour. Give the candidates a last chance to add whatever they may have forgotten to tell you, then decide who is getting back to whom, when. The main difference is that you probe for information about them before you tell them about your job opening. This way you'll get more useful, accurate data during the time you spend together.

Why change the sequence? The problem with explaining the job to the candidates before you ask for information about them is that you give out the clues they need to convince you they are perfect for the job, whether or not they are. Pick up any popular magazine and you'll catch an article on how to interview to get the job you want. The article usually doesn't mention that these interviewing techniques might convince someone to give you a job for which you're not at all suited. So when an interviewer asks for information first, the candidates must present a more honest picture of their skills and qualities. The hirer is then in a much better position to decide whether the candidate is right and is in much more control of the whole selection process.

Find Out What They Are Really Like

You're steps ahead in the game if you can hire people who have an action attitude as their regular method of operation. There's a fairly easy way to find out whether a person gets things done or just spins wheels or talks about it. To elicit such information, however, you must have a clear idea of the job and the qualities it requires. This means a little preparation on your part before the interview. For example, managers often waste everyone's time during an interview by asking the same questions as are on the application or are addressed in the resumé. To avoid this trap, review the job application and resumé ahead of time. Don't use the interview time to repeat what's there. Use this session to obtain the information you can't find on those pieces of paper.

To get at the information that will best help you make the wisest hiring decision, examine the job itself. Figure out what level of education, experience, personal characteristics, and talents you want the person to have. This is the biggest step toward getting the kind of team player you want. The key is to think it through. For example, Joann, an office manager for a firm that manufactures medical equipment, included the following traits on her list for a secretary: "takes initiative," "sets priorities," "is organized," "good communicator," and "team player." The problem Joann ran into was that, in order to determine if the candidates had these qualities, she asked each one outright during the interview. They naturally said yes. Joann felt that she was right back where she started. And she was.

To make this a more useful list and one that will help guide the interview where you need it to go, take one further step. Identify what people actually do if they have the quality or trait you want. An easy way to figure this out is to picture the perfect person in that job. What is he or she doing? What actions are being taken? Or, pretend you are telling someone that you have hired the most terrific person for the position. You are having a wonderful time bragging about what a good job this new employee is doing. What are you telling this other person that the worker is doing?

This exercise will help you identify the actions you expect from the candidate to enable them to do the job right. This way you know exactly what you mean. For instance, Joann's definition of a "good communicator" was someone who can handle two bosses at once and be diplomatic when turning down work from one because she is working on something for the other. In addition, a "good communicator" for her meant that when people ask questions, either in person or over the phone, the employee answers those questions patiently; or, if she doesn't know the answer, finds it and gets back to the questioner. Joann realized that "well organized" meant for her that the secretary's desk is not cluttered, that Joann's calendar is organized in a way that makes sense to her, that her dictation is returned within one working day without errors, and that her grammatical mistakes are corrected.

When defining traits in terms of the actions you expect, your definitions don't have to match anyone else's, or even a dictionary definition. By figuring out what *you* mean, you pay close attention to the standards *you* have. This avoids misunderstandings that can happen when you say to a candidate, "I'm looking for someone with good communication skills. Do you have them?" The interviewee, truly believing he has good communication skills, answers yes. However, his version commonly is very different from yours. For example, the candidate might believe that "good communication skills" means knowing how to create memos and reports, whereas your definition matches the one Joann had. By zeroing in on the actions you want, you make it possible to find out whether a candidate has the action attitude you need.

Look for Action Examples

Lots of managers believe they can't determine an individual's traits during the short period of an interview. But by first deciding what you really want from a person, you pave the way for an efficient and productive interview, even in a limited time frame. Because you have identified those traits that are important to you, you have a head start on creating and preparing the questions that will yield the information you need. Joann prepared for the secretarial interviews by jotting down questions such as, "Do you consider yourself a person who takes the initiative?" She anticipated a yes answer in most cases, so her next question would be, "Please give me an example of when you took the initiative on your last job." By asking for examples Joann created an opportunity to see if both parties were talking about the same thing when referring to "initiative."

Another set of questions to put on your list are the "what" and "why" questions. Joann added to her list, "Do you like the challenge of taking the initiative?" When the interviewee would answer yes again, Joann was ready to follow up with, "Why do you like that challenge?" or "What do you like about the challenge?" These are questions that ask candidates to think, not just give the answers they assume you want. Your job during the interview is to listen very hard to the answers. The best predictor of future behavior is past behavior. It's not foolproof, but it's the best thing you can count on that we know of. By having nailed down exactly what you expect someone to do if he has the traits you want, you can match the answers given with what you want. Dig for actions. Ask for examples. Question why the person likes or dislikes something. When you hear how the candidate handled a situation in the past, see how that fits with your needs and desires for the present and future.

Besides requesting past examples, ask the candidates to respond to some hypothetical situation you have created. Phil wanted someone who would "grab the ball and run with it." Translated into action, Phil wanted an individual who would make decisions by himself as often as possible. When the individual didn't have sufficient information, Phil expected that he would find the person with the information so that the decision could be made. For example, during the interview with Eileen, a candidate for a service rep position with a major appliance distributor, Phil asked her what she would do if a customer wanted something from the warranty that Eileen wasn't sure she could authorize. The answer Phil did *not* want to hear was that Eileen would run to Phil for an answer. Eileen came through with flying colors when she said she would read the relevant parts of the warranty and, if she still couldn't find the answer, she'd call headquarters to see if she could find an answer there. If that failed, she'd make a decision, then run it by Phil for verification.

Phil also wanted an action orientation toward problem solving. He asked Eileen if she had ever been unhappy about something her boss was doing which she felt interfered with getting her job done. Eileen replied that she had. Phil followed with, "Tell me what you did about the situation." Eileen said that she had confronted her boss and had proposed a solution. For Phil, this couldn't have been a better answer. He was an up-front kind of guy who didn't want to pussyfoot about problems, even when they concerned him. He asked Eileen how she handled changes in the office, requesting some examples of how she coped. Again, she answered in a way that matched Phil's requirements.

Phil took advantage of the interview time to really find out how Eileen handled herself in the work environment. Since he had done his homework, he knew the kinds of actions he wanted from his staff. By asking Eileen for examples, plus giving her hypothetical situations and asking "what" and "why" questions, Phil got an accurate picture of how Eileen had handled herself in the past. He could judge how well Eileen would fit the needs of the job. By taking the time to get that kind of information for each job opening, instead of just going with his gut reactions, Phil was building a motivated, action-oriented staff. He was handpicking can-do people right from the start.

Besides selecting action-oriented people from the candidate pool, Phil also sent a message right at the start as to what he expected in terms of motivation and attitude. By citing examples and using hypothetical situations, he gave the interviewees an accurate picture of the job and what would be expected of them.

MAKE NEW MEMBERS PART OF
THE TEAM RIGHT AWAY

Managers want their employees to pull as a team. There are a few things you can do to help this process as new people come on board.

When people join your group, they will feel awkward and pretty much out of place. In the meantime, your established staff will wonder about the new people and how they will fit in. Those first few days are the most important, as you try to have the group move toward working as a team.

New people want to know what job you want them to do. They want to know what your standards are for good performance, and they want to succeed. They are concerned with what you are going to do as well as how other staff members will act and react. They are curious about what their place is in the group and what the roles of the others are. They want to know what the others are like and how they will fit in. And the people already on the team have the same sorts of concerns about the new employees.

Help people get to know each other on a personal basis. It reduces some of the discomfort and creates an avenue for answering some of those questions. You can accomplish this by having a welcoming potluck supper or a happy hour after work. Or, you might just provide the time and doughnuts for a coffee break on the first or second day of work for the new people. Take the time to introduce them to the others they will be working with. Fill them in a little bit on each of these persons, say, by mentioning some special interests each has. Put together a list of names of the people not only in their immediate work group but also those with whom they will interact on a regular basis. Point out their resource persons.

Brief Them on Informal Rules and Customs

You need to do whatever you can to have each newcomer feel—and actually become—an "insider" as quickly as possible. This is reported by employees to be their second highest motivator, after a sense of achievement. The reason for this is that we all want to belong. If people don't feel that they belong, they drop out. This dropping out can be silent or overt: those who silently don't belong don't ever pull with the team; those who are more open about not belonging often cause conflict or leave altogether. If time is not taken to help newcomers feel they belong in the group, a valuable team member may be lost.

Fill new people in on the informal rules that work for your group. When newcomers don't fit in, it's usually because they are unaware of the informal rules. If they don't know about them, they can't follow them and they remain outsiders. Most people eventually pick up on informal rules, but sometimes too late. These new members may not agree with the rules, but at least they will know what they are.

If your work group usually eats lunch together, let new people know that this is the case. Tell them the rules about smoking, eating, breaks, even opening and closing doors. Inform them as to when meetings are and what kind of participation you expect. Fill them in on any special language you have that makes your group different from others. It may surprise you how much of a private language grows within groups the longer they are together. Private jokes are part of that language, as are nicknames for projects or areas. Abbreviations that make your lives run smoother can be a foreign language for newcomers. For example, Judy, a member of a training team, took the initiative at a staff meeting to write down all the abbreviations and slang expressions that were used during the two hours the group was together. She had been putting the list together for a new staff member; everyone was amazed when she produced a glossary with eighty-two items!

If you're not sure what information would be most helpful for a newcomer, ask your most recently hired staff members what they wished they had had in order to have fit in more quickly and comfortably. The sooner newcomers feel like old-timers, the quicker they will pull as part of the team.

Let Them Know They're Important

People all want to do a good job when they start in a new position. To help them, show them they are important. Share the organizational chart with them, and illustrate how they fit in. Explain the major mission of the company or institution, and describe how your department contributes to that mission. One of the most important things you can do is to let new people know how what they do every day contributes to meeting these goals.

To turn your new team members on, remember women and men in today's workplace want to make a contribution to something beyond just making money for the company. Help them see that they are doing this. For example, people involved in manufacturing drugs are helping others get well. Persons who wire computers are helping others get a better handle on complex information. Clerks processing telephone bills are helping others communicate.

Most managers think that people automatically make that link, but many don't. Research done on high-productivity teams shows that this understanding is a key to the function of such groups. We all want to do work that counts, but members of highly productive groups can tell you what their company wants to achieve and how they contribute to reaching that goal. In other words, they know why their work counts. Since new people often wonder how they will contribute, let them know the specific addition they will make to the team. Point out why that contribution is important to you and to the team. Clarify what you expect of them, and fill them in on how you will judge whether they have done it to your satisfaction.

Orient the New Members of the Team

Talk to new team members about the formal work rules as well, and explain how they can get those rules clarified if they have questions or concerns. Establish an atmosphere of open communication right from the start; this contributes to a climate of teamwork and action. When people are free to discuss ideas and concerns, they feel more confident and their self-esteem rises. When people have this feeling, they are more prone to take action and stay motivated.

Make an orientation checklist so you don't have to reinvent the wheel each time you hire someone. Orienting employees from the start—not waiting for them to catch on—is worth every minute and every dollar you spend. When successful, you will have employees sold and on your side.

TRAIN TO ACHIEVE IMMEDIATE RESULTS

People on a new job want to get up to speed as quickly as they can. It's certainly in your best interests to see that they do. Good training is partner to orientation in laying the groundwork for a motivated, productive worker.

Most people eventually learn their job, whether there is formal training or not. But the problem with hit-or-miss training is that it costs a lot more money than does a coordinated effort. With hit-or-miss, costly mistakes can continue for a long time until someone eventually becomes aware of the situation. It takes longer to learn a job on the fly than through a concentrated training effort. There is an old saying: "You pay for a training program whether you intend to or not." So be more efficient and effective. Put some training in place for new people so they can experience success from the start. Nothing gets and keeps someone motivated like success.

Train Your Trainers

Arrange for the success that comes from good training. If you use the buddy system to train new workers, make sure you share your training tips with the individuals you have chosen to do the training. Most people don't know how to train very well, so coach the people to whom you give the responsibility. This way you ensure the results you want and you verify that people in your department are doing the job the way you want it done.

If you use a buddy system, supply a checklist for the trainee as they complete the requirements. The bottom line is that you are the one responsible for making sure the training has taken place and that it has been done to your satisfaction. It's also a good idea to have periodic meetings with each buddy and new worker to check on progress. This shows the new people that you are available and that their success is important to you. It lets the trainers know how critical their help is and that you recognize and appreciate their efforts. Personally follow up, through meetings and observation, to make sure all has transpired according to your desires.

Share the Objectives

The old saying, "If you don't know where you're going, you're bound to end up somewhere else," applies to training. The employees you are training are thinking adults who are helped by knowing that what they are being taught makes sense. If you share with them the objectives of the job, it's much easier for them to assimilate the new material. They are able to more easily make the connection between what they are to do and why it is necessary.

Teach your new employees about your standards. In other words, what will a good job look like? This information is like the foundation of a building. It is the base for shaping and guiding other activity. When coupled with an understanding of the company's and department's goals, this knowledge lets them know quite clearly why the company considers their work important enough to pay them to do it.

Find Out What They Already Know

Teaching adults is a bit different from teaching children. Adults come with some knowledge and skills already in place, so don't waste valuable training time teaching them something they already know. First, find out how their present abilities relate to what you want them to do. The simplest way is to ask. If the employees say they know how to do a particular job, don't irritate them by teaching the skill all over again. Instead, to make sure they will perform the way you want, have them demonstrate it for you to see if you are both speaking the same language and operating the same way. If they tell you they know part of the job, get specific. Then build on what they already know, instead of "re-teaching" everything.

Besides wasting time and irritating people, when you re-teach skills or procedures to people who are already skilled in part of the process, you risk having them drift off when you are on familiar ground. Smart training emphasizes the differences in techniques. If you insist on going over the unnecessary, they can easily miss something important that is different or new. Instead, build on their self-confidence and self-esteem by acknowledging that they have brought something of value to this new job.

Demonstrate With a New Twist

Demonstrations are a terrific way to teach new skills. A teaching mistake that is pretty common, though, is to have trainees look at the demonstration straight on. When this is the case, they see the exact opposite of what they will see when they try to do it themselves. It's a mirror image for them, and often trainees have trouble later on. Instead, have them look over your shoulder as you demonstrate. This way, they will see the procedure exactly the way it will look for them when they later try to duplicate your efforts.

For example, June was getting awfully frustrated because Wendy and Don couldn't seem to conquer the new sterilization procedure. It wasn't complicated, but they just couldn't get the hang of it. The problem was that they had not seen it from the view that they would ultimately be working with. They had faced June straight on as she demonstrated, therefore they kept doing things backwards. When June tried the over-the-shoulder approach, their performance improved immediately.

Of course, this technique works only when the person you are training uses the same dominant hand as you do. If the person you are trying to teach uses the opposite hand, then face them to demonstrate. That way they will have the same perspective when they try to do the job on their own.

When demonstrating some skill, most teachers usually demonstrate, then have the person learn by giving it a try. But put an extra step in there. First, demonstrate what it is that you want them to do. Next, instead of having them try it, ask them to talk you through it and you serve as their hands. This way they can think the whole process through first, without feeling the pressure of making their hands do it right, too. After they have talked you through it, have them do both. Learning sinks in a lot deeper this way.

Taking Advantage of Different Ways of Learning

People have different ways of processing information. Some people must see it to have it sink in. Others can't learn unless they hear the instructions. These differences have absolutely nothing to do with intelligence; it's just preferred ways of learning. Most trainers, unfortunately, have a tendency to teach the way that is most comfortable for them, which causes unnecessary problems. Instead, capitalize on these differences and adjust your training method to match the preferences of your pupils.

Let's take an example. John was trying to get some new computer tricks across to Alex, and John is the type of person who learns best by seeing. He handed Alex the training manual and instructions he had created. He told Alex to read the materials and then they could discuss the job. The problem was that Alex learned better by hearing instructions rather than reading. When Alex didn't catch on fast, John decided that Alex wasn't too bright and didn't learn new things very quickly. He insisted that Alex read the instructions again and again until he understood. In reality, Alex could have been on top of the situation quite rapidly, if only he could have heard the instructions.

To get a handle on how your employees learn best, listen to what they say. If they make statements such as, "This is how I see it," or

"How does it look to you?" you can be pretty sure they learn by seeing. If they are more prone to say, "How does that idea sound to you?" or "What are you hearing me say?" you know they learn better if they hear instructions. Everybody—whether visual or auditory—ultimately learns by doing. That's the basis for the training rule, "See it or hear it, then do it."

Tell Them What and Why

People can learn better and more quickly if they can understand the reasons for doing something. The days of employees blindly doing what the manager wants them to are pretty much gone. You'll help people learn to be competent if you explain the what and why of every step as you give instructions. For example, to teach someone to use a new machine, explain why it is important to turn the valve off each time the machine is stopped. Explain that if you don't, the water leaks, creates a puddle, and makes the machine hard to move again.

Help the job make sense to the individual who is going to be doing it. This aids in decision making when the worker is later faced with some choices if things aren't going perfectly. For instance, if Sally knows that putting the pad on sideways throws the machine off balance, she can make the leap in judgment to recognize that using a pad which is too small will have the same effect. In other words, by arming your employees with in-depth information about why a job is done a certain way, you ensure acceptable end results when workers have to adjust for some less-than-ideal circumstances.

Provide Information on How
They're Doing

"How am I doing?" Feedback has been called the "Breakfast of Champions." It is honest information about what is going well and what isn't. The training time is the perfect point at which to create the communication pattern of filling people in on how things are going. Let employees know what they are doing right. Don't rely on the old motto of, "If you don't hear anything, you can assume it's okay." Make a point of telling employees what in particular they are doing well. This ensures they will continue to do it well. It also builds their self-confidence.

Feedback is not always positive. Make sure you point out when something is not being done correctly, and help the employee immediately to correct the situation. This way, the wrong method doesn't have an opportunity to take hold, and you arrange for the employee to be successful instead. Criticizing someone is difficult at best. Managers have a tendency to shy away from doing it, even during a training situation when an individual expects to hear criticism. On the contrary, take advantage of this time to establish the idea that you will tell them, both when things are going well and when they are off course and need correction.

So often, managers in the training phase don't mention when employees are off the mark because they don't want to undermine their confidence. What really happens is that they allow the employees to think they are doing something correctly, when in fact they aren't. Of course, the employees will continue to do it this way, thinking it is right. The result is that the job does not get done right, and you, the manager, eventually get upset that they have not caught on. In the meantime, the results have been less than perfect and possibly costly. Avoid this by catching errors quickly and set the stage for ultimate success.

Get Them to Talk

So often, managers try to train with one-way communication. They tell or show employees what to do without offering any opportunity for the employees to ask questions, backtrack, or make comments. By opening up the lines of communication during training, you lay the groundwork for good communication all through their careers with you. Employees feel free to discuss questions and issues with you, which not only helps get the job done but boosts their confidence.

Ask the trainees, "What questions do you have?" This is a better way to phrase it than, "Do you have any questions?" because it gives the message that, of course, they do have questions. By letting them know it is natural to have questions, you pave the way for them to not feel awkward or shy about asking. The old saying that, "There's no such thing as a dumb question" applies here. The freer they feel to ask what they need to ask, the better position you are in to get the job done the way you want it done.

Answer your trainees' questions patiently. You may have to phrase your answers or instructions more than one way. For example, a lot of trainers believe they are being very clear when in fact they are not.

Remember, you are probably very familiar with what you are trying to teach. Because of that, you may have a tendency to skip steps or refer to objects by nicknames or abbreviations. Right at the start, announce, "Please ask about anything I say that is confusing or you don't know what I mean."

Investing quality time in training, whether you do it yourself or coach one of your employees in doing it, will pay off over and over. You will reduce the time it takes to get someone up to speed on a job, therefore you will save a lot of time and energy and will reduce mistakes right from the start. People are motivated because they feel competent at their job. They see that doing a good job is important because you have invested time, energy, money, and attention in preparing them. Nothing succeeds like success. Therefore, arrange for your employees to be as successful as they can, as soon as they can be. By having them feel and be successful, you will enjoy a confident work force willing to take action, work around barriers, and get things done.

Chapter 3

Delegate for Guaranteed Results

Delegation can be the key to creating a highly productive, action-oriented team. It also can be the wet blanket that squelches initiative and action. When performed in its truest sense of the word, delegation is sharing authority and responsibility to get a job done. This sharing is the best ticket you've got for building the self-esteem and feeling of accomplishment in your staff that lead to further action. On the other hand, poor delegation eats away at self-esteem and accomplishment. The tone you set as you delegate work lets people know what you really think about their taking risks and moving into action. If you say you want a team that moves into action, but you construct barriers with your delegation style, your staff will not believe you. Remember, when given the choice between believing what is heard and what is seen, people will always go with what they see.

WHY BOTHER TO DELEGATE?

Delegation is really what your job as manager is all about. You manage and control the work actually done by others. Not delegating can be very costly. If you insist on doing most of their work yourself, it is much more expensive. For starters, your salary is undoubtedly higher, possibly much higher, than theirs. Therefore, the time you invest in their work costs more than the time your staff would invest. The second waste of money comes about when you are not doing the job you are paid to do. As manager you have some tasks that no one else in your group can perform. You're the one to make sure the work is coordinated. You tend to financial considerations. Your perspective as manager is invaluable when you join with other managers to share ideas and make plans. You're paid to direct and control the work done in your area. In short, no one else on your team has your bird's-eye view. If you're not doing your job, then the rest of the team will find it difficult to do theirs.

Another invisible cost to not delegating is the potential damage to your career. If you are seen as a manager or supervisor who doesn't delegate, you may well be passed over for promotions, because the load only gets heavier the higher you go. If you are seen as one of those managers who doesn't use available resources, including people, your career could come to a sudden stop.

By delegating work, obviously more work can get done. Through your coordinating efforts, the group can operate and feel like a team. Sharing responsibilities through delegation offers opportunities for your staff members to become more skilled at their jobs. It can be a wonderful chance to learn and get good at something new. By building the capabilities of your team members, you triple the return on your investment in them. By providing delegation opportunities, employee confidence gets a boost; you are giving the message that you have confidence in them. Delegation shows confidence in a very public way. With skillful delegation, you help employees achieve, which is the ultimate motivator.

SEVEN BARRIERS TO DELEGATION

When managers think of delegating some work or responsibility, they sometimes get cold feet. They can come up with a truckload of reasons why delegating is not such a hot idea.

It Takes Too Much Time

One common reservation is that it takes too much time to delegate work. Initially, delegating work certainly can take more time than if you were to do the job yourself. However, think about the long haul. Are you always able to do the job every time it needs to get done, or is it better to have someone skilled and available do that job?

For example, at the end of each month, Rick needed to submit to his boss a monthly activity report which reflected the work done by his marketing staff. He wrote the report based on information submitted by his staff. It wasn't anything fancy—just a short summary of the month. Rick finally realized that he would save himself a pile of time by delegating this task to his assistant, Tony. All he needed to do was to train Tony in the format the boss wanted and to explain what activities fell into which categories. He trained Tony to judge which items were appropriate to include and which were not. Now Tony does the draft and runs it by Rick each month. Instead of Rick's using up two hours each month, he now spends fifteen minutes.

If you find yourself reluctant to delegate because you think it will take less time to do the job than to teach someone else, run some numbers. Figure out how often the job needs to be done. How long will it take you to train someone else to do it to your satisfaction? If it still is more time efficient for you to do it, as with a one-time shot, then of course do it. Often, however, managers underestimate how much time a particular job takes or how frequently it is done. It's more than likely that the job can be delegated.

If You Want a Job Done Right,
Do It Yourself

Lots of individuals who reach management positions believe that if they want a job done right, they have to do it themselves. This sense of responsibility is probably part of the philosophy that got them into the position they hold. However, tremendous damage can be done to the team and the team members' motivation by this position.

Consider what this statement really communicates. In essence, you are saying, "I don't trust you as people who are able to accomplish important tasks. I am the only one who can perform well here." If you are striving to create a bias for action, this attitude douses cold water on your attempts. People don't take action unless they feel capable and confident. Even if employees initially felt capable and confident, through your lack of delegation they can lose their confidence and be hesitant to act. A side effect of not delegating is growing resentment and lack of loyalty.

Explore whether this feeling actually is true. Ask yourself, "If I am the only one in the bunch who is capable of executing a job correctly, why did I hire these folks in the first place?" And, "Even if I didn't hire them, why am I continuing to pay their salaries if they're not capable?" If truly you are the only person in the group who can do anything correctly, you have fertile ground for training, coaching, and cleaning out, if necessary.

It Takes Planning

Exactly. One of your jobs—a skill you need to model for your employees—is to plan. Delegating work is a great way to demonstrate this skill. Effective delegation requires some advance work, whereas haphazard delegation yields disappointing results. Without planning, you waste your resources and accomplish little. When delegating a job, you have the ideal opportunity to coach your staff in the art of planning and organizing. Once you train them in these techniques, you'll find they are used on a regular basis, not only for special assignments but also for the regular, day-to-day flow. The simple planning model provided in Chapter 11 is a sound base.

Joe, a manager in a marketing division, wanted to delegate special projects to his staff, but no one volunteered. One reason was that he didn't plan very well, and the people who in the past had taken a chance and volunteered found themselves on the receiving end of some poorly thought-out situations. In addition, Joe had never shared any information on how to plan so that the actions could be pulled off in a reasonable time while still fitting in with the normal work. A lot of these projects would have heaped glory on the people who took them, but he never had any takers. His employees felt they had a full work load already. They considered taking on these projects, but in spite of the benefits, they felt they would be overwhelmed. Joe cured this problem by showing how planning can take away that sense of impending overload by cutting the job into small bites and adding a task or two a day to get the extra work done without too much pain. Once he did this, Joe had a much happier, more successful work group that had a good time with the extra projects. Part of his success was directly traceable to the planning he demonstrated as he assigned those extra jobs.

It's Too Hot

At times there are jobs you simply cannot delegate. They may be politically hot items. Often, they involve key information you can't share with employees. Sometimes, it's simply a case of the buck stops with you. These reasons are all legitimate. The danger, however, is that managers often place issues or projects in this category when they really don't belong there. Also, be careful when you hear yourself say that something is too important to delegate. Why is it too important? What is it about that particular project that renders your employees not good enough?

They Might Do a Better Job Than I Would

Lots of managers are timid about delegating work because they are afraid their employees will do a better job than they can. Instead, what a terrific way for you to look good! Show that you're smart and savvy enough to hire competent people, then manage them so well that they do lots of things excellently. The main reaction others will have when your group does well is not to criticize you but instead to give you the credit for unleashing all that motivation and skill.

By its definition and nature, the job of manager moves you from the area of technical skills into the managerial arena. Sometimes, people in managerial positions treat management skills lightly. They don't respect their job and the talent it takes in the same way they respect their technical skills. The talent it takes to manage a group of workers well is just as distinct a set of skills as those needed to design a building, produce a chemical formula, create a computer program, or build an airplane. Getting work done through other individuals is not an easy task. Pray that your people are technically better than you are and can outstrip your technical performance. They are the ones doing the technical jobs on a regular basis, not you. You're doing your management job on a regular basis. If you were able to outshine them in technical skills, you wouldn't be doing your management job.

Don't Want to Let Go of the Good Jobs

It's certainly a temptation to keep the juicy projects on your desk. They're fun, and often there's an appealing reward. One problem with this, however, is that an upper-level management that wants a motivated work force doesn't get very excited about its managers operating this way. Holding on to projects and doing them yourself doesn't allow you to do your management job. This gets noticed. You're supposed to be managing, not doing. Shine through your people, instead. What a boon to them to be given a project that can showcase their abilities.

If you always keep the good work for yourself, the enthusiasm of your staff for other assignments can certainly be dampened. By not sharing the fun, by not giving them highly visible, high-reward projects, you will severely hinder the quality and quantity of their output. You really can be a double winner with these high-appeal projects. When you share them, your employees feel more committed, rewarded, and loyal. They put out their best, not only on the special jobs but on the routine ones as well. You bask in the reflected glory of their great performance.

Don't Want to Give Up Power and Control

Roberta was a fairly new manager with the marketing division of a retail operation. She was very satisfied because her office appeared to be the hub of activity for her group. Every few minutes a staff member or colleague would pop in her door and ask a question about a project's progress or status. She would consult her well-organized, handy-dandy project book she had created, and provide answers with words of wisdom. This stream of activity never stopped. Roberta was pretty impressed with herself.

One day, while patting herself on the back for being so well informed and being such a respected resource, Roberta had a sharp jolt. The idea dawned on her that people possibly weren't coming to her for information and advice because they valued her words of wisdom. Her office was a hub of activity only because she failed to share the information that could be helpful to others. She learned a very valuable lesson as she gritted her teeth and released her grasp on the information.

The change in her staff was remarkable. Their confidence grew. Their decisions were better because they had access to all the information, not just bits and pieces meted out. The work atmosphere improved, and the relationship between Roberta and her staff became less distant. This allowed for much more meaningful communication, which led to increased productivity.

TEN WAYS TO GUARANTEE THE RESULTS YOU WANT

Unfortunately, delegation is often treated as a fishing expedition or a treasure hunt. Goals are not articulated clearly, and there are a lot of false starts, groping, and nonproductive work in an effort to discover what is to be accomplished. A manager who says, "I'll know the result I want when I see it," is wasting considerable employee time, energy, motivation, and money. Without well-defined goals and standards, futile attempts will be made. More often than not, those attempts will be rejected, and discouragement will grow.

Without goals, you lose confidence in your employees' abilities, and they resent your continual rejection of their efforts. How much less frustrating for everyone if you establish goals and standards up front. Then, the effort can be focused and efficient, instead of resembling a line dangled in the water with the hope of some reasonable results.

Zero In on Your Goals

As you formulate your goals, nail down what you want to accomplish in doing this job. How does it fit with your company's goals and objectives? Follow the guidelines for goal setting and make sure the goals are measurable and specific. For example, Helen, a manager of information systems, wanted to offer training and backup for the myriad personal computers popping up in offices all over her organization. She wanted to do a needs assessment to determine how her department could be of service. But her original goal of, "Contact some users about their computer needs," didn't qualify as a well-stated objective. When she rephrased it to, "Interview twenty division chiefs within the next two months with a set of questions regarding their needs for personal-computer services from our office," Helen was able to communicate a much clearer picture to Donna, the associate she wanted to accomplish the task.

Helen's vision of what should happen, when expressed as a vague statement such as her first version, was quite different from that of

Donna's. Donna had conjured up visions of interviews conducted nationwide by extensive survey, involving regression analysis and producing a major thesis on the results. Helen's desires were a bit more modest. She wanted Donna to interview twenty managers, with the results reflected in a two-page report. Only after she rephrased her goal in specific terms did Donna have a better idea of what was to be done. Therefore, use specifics to nail down your version of your goal. This way, you clear the path for success right from the start.

Keep Control Without De-Motivating

The delegation principle of "leave the employee alone" strikes terror into the hearts of many managers. Leaving your subordinates alone does not mean abdication, however. It does mean not sitting on their shoulders as they try to do the job you have given them to do. It means trusting them to do a good job without hounding them. When you delegate well, you establish with your employees at the outset the mutually acceptable communication patterns you both will follow.

Decide, as you think a project through, how much communication you'll need to feel comfortably in control without strangling employee motivation. If this type of responsibility is new to the employees, you probably will establish more frequent checkpoints than you would with individuals who are more experienced. In our previous example, since Donna was fairly new to this sort of project, Helen wanted to review the questions to be asked and the list of interviewees before contact was made. When the interviewing was completed, she wanted to see a rough draft of the report. With a more experienced worker, Helen probably would have been content with just seeing the final report. The point is to identify what plan makes you comfortable, then stick with it.

The principle of leaving employees alone to do the job underlines the honoring of time between checkpoints. During the intervals, don't constantly ask, "How's it going?" or, "Let me look over what you have so far." Or, "I double-checked the work I saw lying on your desk." You may think you're showing interest. Employees will think you're meddling and showing distrust. You've given them a job to do; let them do it. Your plan should have adequate checks and balances built in, to allow you to catch and deter possible difficulties. Do it on scheduled time, though. Honor that agreement in order to communicate your confidence and respect.

Be Available as a Resource

A manager may have a communication plan in mind that doesn't call for a lot of interaction during the project, but employees request more frequent checkpoints. Some managers reply, "No, that's not necessary," convinced that this response is a way to communicate confidence in the staff's abilities. For the employees it feels like desertion. When your employees ask you to serve as a resource, generally it is because they genuinely feel your guidance is needed. They may feel unsure about some aspects of the project or their ability to perform.

Instead of conveying a message of confidence when you turn down such a request, more often you communicate a lack of interest and a disinclination to help. By not giving people the time or help requested, you withhold resources from them that they believe are necessary to complete the project successfully. Be available to your staff as much as they need you.

If employees request fewer checkpoints than you have specified, consider their argument. If it's valid and you can live with their plan, of course do it. However, if you really wouldn't be comfortable with the plan they offer, stick to your guns. You are, after all, the person ultimately responsible for the project and you need to stay on top of it.

Select the "Right" Person

To overcome the hurdles of delegation, select the "right" person for each job. As you decide who is the right person, take into account each employee's interest, training, time, and ability. If someone is very interested in an area and would be the most enthusiastic person for that job, but hasn't a lick of time, that individual may not be the "right" person. Likewise, the person with the time but no interest may not be your first choice, either.

Take the time to make a quick list of the abilities, training, and interest as well as the time that's needed to make the project a success. Then consider who might fill the bill. Too often managers go the other way and get someone in mind, then try to make that person's qualifications fit the task. Thorough assessment of what you need will help you answer the top question in everyone's mind when given an assignment, "Why me?" This early assessment can help you do a sales job on the person, and it's another golden opportunity to reinforce the successes and talents of your employees. These are all ingredients to add to the pot of increased risk-taking behavior.

"Make" the Right Person for the Job

If there are employees you feel would increase their skills by taking on new assignments, or there are only a few people who have the time at the moment, it's possible to "make" them be the right people for the job. Figure out what instruction or training they will need, also what resources you can provide to make the training happen. For example, employees' project-management skills might not be honed finely enough for you to have full confidence in their ability. Consider what it will take to get them up to speed. Does it involve coaching from you? Reading a book? Seeing a tape? Taking a ten-week course?

Determine if any of these steps are feasible. If it will take a ten-week course to get the skills up to snuff, but the project deadline is one month from today, obviously this is not the best possible choice. On the other hand, if seeing a tape, coupled with coaching from you, can be accomplished within a week, you'll have a double winner on your hands. Not only do you get the delegated project completed, but you will have used the job as a vehicle for developing skills that can be used several times over.

Don't Dump Jobs on Employees

Be careful to avoid dumping jobs on employees who are cheerful about taking on such unappealing projects. You run the risk of burning them out so that they are no longer willing to do these awful jobs; chances are they will become reluctant even to take on the good ones.

Every operation has chores that everyone hates. These can be drawing up the month-end report, getting rid of the trash in the closet before the government inspectors come, babysitting with the midnight run, or reviewing the reports and correcting them, or even every rush job that comes into the place. If you're lucky, you have individuals on your staff who don't mind—or at least say they don't mind—doing these things. They do them well, with no complaining, and the work is done when you need to have it done. But what do you usually do with people like this? Most managers tend to give them all the bad-news jobs. Their reward for being a good team player is more of the same. Then, one day, these cooperative, productive employees balk at just about every-thing you ask. They end up resentful about even routine work. Unfor-tunately, managers often assume that these employees' attitudes have changed and they believe that it's more proof you can't get good help anymore.

These managers neglect to look at the part they have played. When a job is unpleasant, everyone has to take a turn at the wheel. Split up the nasty jobs among the staff, even though in the short run it causes you a few headaches. It evens out in the end, and you don't wreck the motivation of your best workers. When you can arrange for sharing, do so. Don't reward good performance with crummy job assignments.

Share Responsibility and Power

I'll bet you can recall some times when you were given responsibility to do a job but not the authority to do it. As you delegate, grant your employees the power to be successful. This is another way of building commitment. Do they need signature approval for computer time? Will they require extra clerical help? Do they need entry into confidential data? Determine what it takes to get the project completed, then make sure they don't have to run to you constantly for permission or re-sources.

As a safeguard for your managerial comfort, determine the boundaries of their authority. This can mean a signature limit of $5,000, temporary help for one month, or clearance into restricted files for two weeks. Identify the limits and you keep ultimate control with you, where it belongs. You also prevent potentially embarrassing or awkward situa-tions for employees while you pave a way to success.

Delegate Gradually

If delegating is a relatively new experience for your work group, take it one step at a time—for their sake as well as yours. You don't want to scare yourself or them. Everyone is going to feel a bit unsure, so by delegating and increasing responsibility gradually, you'll find a success-ful outcome is more likely.

Be patient with yourself and with them. Delegation is like any new skill; it takes time, persistence, and learning from mistakes. As you delegate, analyze what you did right and what could have been done better. As mistakes happen, keep people involved. Don't snatch the task away. Say those six little words, "Where do we go from here?" Eventually, everyone will get comfortable with the shared responsibility.

Delegate the Whole Project

If you can, hand over the whole project. "Owning" a job is a great motivator. Taking a job from start to finish adds to a worker's self-esteem and opens the door for more action. Certainly, some projects are simply too large or require input and effort from too many sources to be the exclusive property of just one person. But try to adhere to this idea even when that is the case. Give people specific chunks of a job they can claim as their own. When planning, take extra care to avoid overlaps or gaps. High on the irritation scale is being given a job, doing one's best, then finding out someone else was given the same responsibility. From a managerial point of view, that is a costly mistake. The next time you delegate pieces of a larger project to these individuals, you'll run the danger that they will believe they don't need to be as thorough or careful as usual because they will assume that you have double-assigned again. When planning, make an extra effort to avoid duplication of effort.

Also high on the irritation scale is working one's utmost, meeting the deadline, and then finding out the project can go no further because the next step was never assigned. This, too, serves to dampen enthusiasm for the next project. People get discouraged, don't try as hard, and become sloppy about deadlines, believing that it doesn't matter anyway.

Gain Commitment by Involving People in the Process

Delegation can be the perfect coaching tool. It is an ideal opportunity to share your thinking as you make decisions. Provide your staff with the chance to incorporate their input. They may have information to add or subtract to your plan. Possibly, they will also given it even more thought than you, since they will be held accountable for the result. Your employees may have more information or greater insights than you because they are closer to the job. Remember, you don't have all the answers just because you are boss. This is another instance when you can allow the staff to shine and impress them with the fact that you are smart enough to ask their advice.

Together, review your version of your goals. Possibly, they will be able to refine them even further. Share your assumptions about their abilities, training, interest, motivation, and time availability. They may have some surprises for you—pleasant and not so pleasant. You may think they want to learn how to work with micros, and they really may not be interested. You may think they need bottom-up training in project management, and they may inform you that they already did quite a bit of that on a different job.

Overall, your staff may contribute some valuable points that didn't occur to you. You picked these people to do these jobs for a reason. Use the skills they have to offer, right from the start.

PROCEED WITH A COUPLE OF CAUTIONS

There are some common problems that can crop up as you delegate. With a little warning, you can prevent them from causing trouble. First, both you and your staff may have invested highly in this project, so you both keep your fingers in the pie. The manager is the bigger sinner in this situation. Stick to your agreed-upon communication schedule and sit on your hands if you must, but keep your distance and your agreements.

Second, expectations sometimes get switched and people forget to tell each other. This change can be very subtle while at other times new information is dropped like a bomb. Make sure you keep everyone informed in a timely way, so that they all know the game—or at least some of its rules—has changed.

A third sin managers often commit is to start the ball rolling before the task is delegated. They neglect to communicate this to the delegatee, and the person to whom the job is given puts a plan in place and starts to implement when, in fact, the manager has already done the same thing. The problem is that the manager has taken a different tack, which results in confusion for all concerned. This happened in our previous example. Donna was given the assignment to complete the computer needs assessment, but Helen, the manager, already had mentioned to four division chiefs that they would be on the interview list. They were looking forward to participating in this project; however Donna didn't know anything about it because Helen had forgotten to mention it to her. They were not on Donna's list. The result was that not only did the job look poorly planned and executed to others but those four division chiefs were irritated and disappointed.

By carefully delegating, you use the top motivators available to you as a manager. You help your people achieve, you display confidence in their abilities, and you draw on them as valuable resources. By being clear about the goals, you ensure that the job you want accomplished is in fact accomplished. In selecting the "right" person for the job, you get a double return on your investment. In delegating well, you increase the skill levels of your staff. When you establish a communication pattern and process, you guarantee that you will always be on top of the project. The best benefit of all is that when people are given the responsibility, the resources, and the authority to do a job well, they come through with increased dedication and action orientation.

Chapter 4

A Mistake Is Just Another Way of Doing Things

Did you know that blue jeans, rubber tires, and the common safety mask are the results of mistakes? Were you aware that Scotch tape, the TV mini-series, and the fact that Ivory soap floats fall into the same category? Yet, what do you think of when you hear the word *mistake?* Do you think of a good thing that might have resulted, or do you envision failure, irresponsibility, trouble, disaster? I've asked this question of thousands of people in my seminars, and I can count on one hand the number who see the success side of mistakes rather than the failure side.

TURN YOUR THINKING AROUND

Your attitude about mistakes can make or break the action-oriented climate you are trying to establish. The way you respond to the mistakes you and your staff make will determine whether you have a dynamic, action-oriented group or a stagnant, safety-driven team. To create a climate in which employees are willing to take chances and be motivated, you must not only accept mistakes but actually encourage them. If people aren't making some mistakes along with their successes, it means they are sticking too close to the safe and sure or they're not moving at all.

In the 1840s, Levi Strauss intended to take advantage of the business boom accompanying the gold rush. He sailed to San Francisco with several rolls of canvas that he hoped to sell as material for tents and wagon covers. While he was trying to sell his canvas and having little success at it, one of the miners told him he had made a mistake. He said that what the miners really needed were pants that could stand up to the rugged life they were leading. Instead of feeling bad about his mistake, Strauss turned the potential disaster into a winner for everyone. "Levis" have existed in essentially the same form for the past 130 years.

Charles Goodyear made the mistake of spilling a mixture of Indian rubber and sulphur on a hot stove while he was working on another project. What was the result? Goodyear looked for the good instead of bemoaning the bad, and today vulcanized rubber moves America along the highways. Likewise, if someone hadn't bothered to move forward with failed ribbon material and turn it into a failed bra cup, we wouldn't now have the common safety mask that protects so many workers every day.

If employees aren't making mistakes, chances are they aren't trying new processes, investigating new markets, or forging new paths in product or service lines. If your employees aren't trying new ways of doing things and moving from the safety of the tried-and-true, your division undoubtedly is stuck in place or maybe even losing ground. If this is happening in your area, look for two possible obstacles: them or you.

Motivating Through Mistakes

No one likes to make mistakes; most of us generally view them as unpleasant experiences. People have been taught from the time they were children that mistakes are bad and should be avoided at almost all cost. So, we all learned that one way to avoid mistakes is to avoid anything that isn't safe and predictable. When people make mistakes, they usually say nasty, discouraging things to themselves. Sometimes, other people get ugly, too.

Most of us have spent a good part of our lives trying to avoid mistakes. This is very powerful conditioning that can paralyze us as we make our way through the vast number and great variety of decisions and risks that make up our world. In the realm of business, it's difficult enough for employees to face themselves when they make a mistake. If it isn't supportive, your response has the potential of killing any future desire to take chances or try something new.

Managers, in their desire to run a productive, well-controlled shop, often unintentionally punish employees for trying new approaches. In doing this, they discourage risk-taking action or do away with it altogether. Think of how the world would be different today if Levi Strauss's "boss" had jumped on him for not doing a decent market analysis, had sent the canvas back to inventory, and had shipped Levi back home to Bavaria? Levi Strauss & Co.'s advertising alone provides a comfortable living for lots of people.

Unfortunately, actions can be devastating even when discouragement isn't the intention. For example, David, a stockroom employee in a small company, tried a new method of inventory control. The mistake he made was forgetting to mention the change to the other shift. Kurt, his manager, decided to "fix" the mistake by posting a notice on the bulletin board announcing that David had tried a new method of control but that it didn't work because David had forgot to mention it to anyone else. Kurt's notice stated that the procedure would be back the way it used to be by midnight the next evening. Kurt then had David stay overtime and restore the entire stockroom to the way it was.

Kurt believed he was simply solving a problem and then communicating the solution of that problem to the people who needed to know. In other words, he was doing his job as manager. David was embarrassed and angry about the way Kurt handled the matter. The result? David didn't try another new idea while still working at that company. He left not too long after the incident, and everyone was very sorry to see him go. He had been one of the best and most motivated individuals in the company.

People get excited when they can try new things safely. When they get jumped on or humiliated if the new approach or product doesn't work perfectly the first time, they're not going to stick their necks out again. The result is reduced motivation, not only for those employees but for the rest of the group as well. In David's case, his fellow workers found out through David's experience that they had better be very careful if they want to try out something new. Therefore their area is one of the least creative and productive in the plant.

To remove some of the barriers to intelligent risk taking, listen to yourself and watch your actions. What are your reactions when employees make a mistake? Do you get angry, worried that your management will be upset? Do you look at the mistake as a first step in the process of creating something good? Do you encourage employees to keep going? Do you snatch the project away from them, assuming that leaving it in their hands will only make matters worse? Pay attention. You may learn that your staff lacks a motivated attitude because of how you react when they make a move and when they make a mistake.

Capitalizing on Mistakes

People don't set out to make mistakes, yet from the reactions of some managers, you'd think the sole intention of the person making the mistake was to make their lives miserable. I bet that every decision you or your employees make is the best decision that can be made at the time, taking into consideration the available information and resources. I further wager that, given identical circumstances, not one decision in your or anyone else's life would be different.

It's easy to stumble into the trap of sometimes seeing another person's choice as a mistake because you would have chosen a different option. Maybe you have more or different information. Perhaps your experiences steer you in another direction. You can do yourself and your staff an enormous favor by keeping in mind what a very successful executive, quoted in the book *Leaders*,[1] said: "A mistake is just another way of doing things."

At times, an employee's choice of "just another way of doing things" does not contribute to accomplishing your goals. Do I suggest that you let the mistake ride and ignore it because the employee didn't set out to make that mistake knowingly? Of course not. But I am suggesting that sometimes, while trying to do a good job of managing, you get into a negative frame of mind when your staff makes mistakes. It's hardly a surprise. Not only were you conditioned from the time you were small to think of mistakes as something unproductive and bad, but that conditioning keeps getting reinforced. Even the dictionary defines *mistake* as an event not to be treasured:

[1]Warren Bennis and Burt Nanus (New York: Harper & Row, 1985), p. 69.

Mistake (mi stāk') *n.,v.,* an error caused by a lack of skill, attention, knowledge, etc. **2** a wrong judgment or idea—*v.t.,* **3** to regard or identify wrongly.[2]

Calling something an "error" doesn't help either, because the dictionary defines an error as "a sin or wrongdoing"!

Smart management capitalizes on mistakes. It encourages smart mistakes. It uses mistakes as an opportunity to help employees develop into even more valuable staff members.

Maintaining an Action Attitude

Sometimes, in your effort to be a good manager, you believe it's your duty to criticize employees when mistakes are made, so that they will not repeat them. At times, you may feel it's in the best interest of all concerned to take people off particular jobs or projects. Instead of criticizing or snatching the project away when a mistake surfaces, use that incident to coach your employees in problem solving, enhance their self-esteem, and build their risk-taking muscles.

The smart action when a mistake happens is to ask the question, "Where do we go from here?" This is the time to remedy the situation, not to stew, worry or blame. John, a good friend who at the time was manager of training at a large corporation, taught me this principle.

He had hired a consultant to put together a program for the senior officers in his company. John made a mistake by not staying on top of the situation. Two weeks before the meeting was to take place, John discovered that the consultant wasn't going to be able to come through. He fired him and grabbed the phone to call me.

He asked me to help pull him out of the fire by giving him some suggestions for making the meeting a success. As I worked out a plan with him, I realized that he didn't seem flustered or upset. This surprised me, because I knew how important this meeting was for John. When I mentioned this to him, he shared his philosophy about mistakes. He said he had learned a long time ago that he could fret and agonize over the consequences of a mistake while making no move to remedy the situation, or he could get to work and try to fix the problem. John claimed that he'd learned worrying got him nothing but headaches, ulcers, and trouble. The worst part about worrying without taking

[2]*The Random House Dictionary* (New York: Random House, Inc., 1980), p. 564.

action was that the problem didn't have a chance of being solved. Working on a solution at least gave him a chance to pull the situation out of the fire.

At the time this sounded like the sort of thing someone says to sound resourceful. I was skeptical that this mistake would turn out well. However, John called me two weeks later (after the meeting) and said that the senior officers loved the way he had pulled off the meeting and even gave him a bonus as a reward. Obviously he wouldn't have been such a hit if he hadn't jumped right into the mess and done the best he could with what he had to work with, instead of moaning and beating himself because he had made a mistake.

Not long after that incident, I was in John's office and my eye caught a poster hanging on his wall. It showed a crowd with a single person in front of the group. The saying on it was, "When they're running you out of town, get to the front and make it look like a parade." He has parlayed this way of operating into what we can all agree is success. This experience taught me the value of those six little words, "Where do we go from here?"

LEARN FROM MISTAKES

The second question to ask, after "Where do we go from here?," is "What went wrong and can we prevent it from happening in the future?" By tracing errors you uncover possible problems in the system. Maybe adequate resources weren't available. Maybe enough information wasn't gathered. Maybe the employee's decision-making skills weren't developed enough. Whatever the reason, it's difficult to practice prevention if you don't know why the incident or "failure" occurred.

For example, Jill ordered the wrong uniforms for the door attendants at the hotel for which she worked. Instead of just letting it go and re-ordering the correct uniforms, Jill did some investigation. It turned out that the order form from the company had a misprint. Several other buyers had run into the same problem with this company. Because Jill took the time to search out why she had made a mistake, several hotels saved money and the uniform manufacturing company was eternally grateful.

Thomas Edison perfected the technique of treating mistakes as wonderful learning experiences. A storage battery he was creating had fifty thousand experiments behind it before it was a success. In response to a remark an observer made regarding the lack of results, Edison replied, "Results? Why, I have gotten a lot of results. I know fifty thousand things that won't work."

Mistakes can sometimes be an expensive training ground. That's all the more reason to learn from mistakes instead of sweeping them under the corporate carpet. Take advantage of mistakes when they happen. For example, a manager at one of the Big Three automobile companies made a $250,000 mistake. Fully believing he would be fired, he was amazed and relieved to be kept on. The rationale? His boss said, "I just paid a quarter of a million dollars for his training. I guarantee he'll never make that mistake again. Why should I let another company take advantage of that?"

KEEP THE EMPLOYEE INVOLVED

Many times, in your effort to correct an error made by your employees, you grab responsibility away from them, fix the difficulty, and share with them very little information about the results. You may believe that you simply are being efficient and perhaps rescuing them from a tough situation. But in spite of possible good intentions, when you snatch the problem away, you send employees the message that you don't believe they are capable of handling the situation or creating a reasonable solution to the problem.

To further your goal of creating an action team and building an action attitude, keep them on the project until the problem is fixed. Don't grab the ball just because they fumbled. Employee mistakes provide you with ideal opportunities to coach them in decision making and problem solving. They can learn from you as you both work to pull the situation out of the fire. If you treat mistakes and their remedies as teaching experiences, employees will learn not to be afraid to try something new, even though they realize it has an 85 percent chance of not being right the first, second, or maybe even third time. They will apply what they learn each time to the next situation they run up against.

LOOK FOR UNEXPECTED
SUCCESSES

Sometimes, in fixing what you believe is a mistake, you stumble on a formula for success. When Fred Silverman took over at ABC, he realized that the network had already sunk a large amount of money into a project called "Roots." Believing it was a poor investment, he wanted to cut his losses. Silverman decided the best way to accomplish that goal was to broadcast all the segments of the show during a one-week period instead of dragging it out. In fixing what he believed to be a mistake, he began the highly profitable concept of the mini-series.

Scotch tape as we know it today is the result of what happened when the 3M Company cleaned up a mistake. In fact, the adhesive tape even got its name from the incident. In 1925, the fad for two-toned cars was developing. Automobile manufacturers needed a way to create a sharp line where the two colors met on the body of the car. In response to their need, 3M created and produced a wide piece of tape with adhesive on each edge, but with none in the center of the strip. When the tape wouldn't stick to the car bodies, one of the painters told a 3M salesman to take it back to his "Scotch" bosses and put adhesive all over the tape, not just on the edges. The company took the worker's advice and even named it for the "Scotch" bosses he tried to insult.

MISTAKES ARE PART OF DOING BUSINESS

People of action and accomplishment realize that mistakes are going to happen. In an address to the 1986 graduating class of Virginia Tech, Neil Armstrong, the first man to walk on the moon, challenged the group to "accept the fact that you'll make some world-class mistakes." People who don't stand still take that into account as they figure their batting average or, in some cases, golf score. Walter Hagen, one of the finest golfers of all times, had a solid attitude regarding mistakes: "I expect to make at least seven mistakes each round. Therefore, when I make a bad shot, I don't worry about it. It's just one of those seven."

Fifteen percent of the time you can count on mistakes happening when you or your employees take action, no matter what you do to prevent them. Another 15 percent of the time everything will be perfect—none of you could put a monkey wrench in the works no matter how hard you tried. The remaining 70 percent of the time you will scoot up and down a continuum, with some risks turning out better than others—but all turning out positively—depending on the information at hand, available resources, and good fortune. The bottom line is that you and your team can expect to be right and have a workable plan for risk 85 percent of the time.

Many people are skeptical when they hear that percentage. Test it out yourself. Keep track of the actions of you and your team. Pay attention to the risks you take, the decisions you make. Be sure to include everyday goals as well as spectacular results. See if your average doesn't match these figures; most people find they do.

One reason people doubt this statistic is because they concentrate on what went wrong, not what went right. Think about it. If you do ninety-nine jobs correctly in a day and have to bite the bullet on one, which job is it you dwell on long after you've left the office? While as rational, thinking individuals we all answer yes to the question, "We all make mistakes, correct?", deep in our hearts lurks a voice that says, "But not me." That's a leftover from way back when, and it is very hard to shake. Keep a record for a while of the chances you and your team take, check which ones turn out well and which ones don't, and you'll probably be quite surprised and pleased with the results.

SOME MISTAKES ARE WORTH A LOT

Every now and then, a positive side effect comes from that 15 percent when mistakes happen. Ivory was just another soap on the market, with nothing to make it outstanding, until someone made a mistake. One of the workers left a batch of the soap in the stirring machine too long. This created air pockets in the hardened bar so that it floated. Ivory quickly became distinguished as the only soap on the market with this feature. In fact, the floating action was so popular that Procter & Gamble had the machines adjusted permanently to capitalize on that mistake. The company parlayed the error into a success that has been floating around for more than 100 years.

Creating an action attitude among your team requires first that you shake off your ingrained reaction that says mistakes are negative and wrong. Your next job is to cultivate that attitude in your employees. To help switch their perspective, share stories of mistakes that turned out well. Tell tales of mistakes that have happened in your company, with your team, in your division, or that you have made. When you talk about these mistakes, do it in a positive way by pointing out how they were fixed and how progress just doesn't happen without people's trying things and making some mistakes along the way. You're the one to set the tone. By talking about mistakes as productive tries on the way to success, you let your employees know you want them out there taking intelligent chances and displaying a willingness to take some risks.

Dealing with mistakes in this way sends the message that mistakes can be transformed into successes. Sometimes, as you work to fix mistakes, good things happen unexpectedly. At times, mistakes are valued because they are the natural fallout of the many tries it often takes to reach a different goal, as in the case of Edison. By showing acceptance and encouragement of mistakes, you'll mobilize your staff to move along the road to action.

Chapter 5

Motivate With Problem Solving

No matter how well you delegate, how good you are at selecting employees, how solid their planning skills, or how great your training efforts, problems will appear. What you do with these problems sets the level of action your employees will take and indicates how much they will accomplish. When problems appear, one way to handle them is to leap in and dictate a solution, hoping it will get carried out to your satisfaction. Another, more productive approach is to make the employees partners in getting the problems solved. When you use a partnership approach, employees are much more committed to the solution. In addition, they build their problem-solving skills so that you won't always have to be involved in the future when the inevitable problems appear. By having the employees work with you, you ensure they learn a method for solving problems that you can agree with, so as to avoid unpleasant surprises down the road for either of you.

By keeping employees involved every step of the way, you continue to build their confidence and self-esteem. This leads to more action on their part. By remaining with the problem and being an integral part of the resolution, they can learn from the situation and be able to prevent difficulties in the future.

Getting employees involved in the problem-solving process may contradict some things you've heard about good management. Aren't you supposed to be the one who earns your bucks by solving problems? Isn't that supposed to be one of the particular jobs of a manager? Yes, it is. But, that doesn't imply you have to have all the answers. It means that you have to facilitate the problem solving in the most efficient and effective way.

Holding yourself accountable for coming up with all the answers is a big mistake. First, even a superhuman manager doesn't have all the answers. Second, you're often too far removed from the nitty-gritty circumstances surrounding a problem to have all the information you need for the best solution. One of your jobs as manager is to make sure problems get resolved. Employees are much more committed to ideas they come up with than to ones you thought of. An employee's lack of commitment to a solution can result in its not being implemented thoroughly, or not being put into place at all. By making all the decisions to solve problems, you actually interfere with the most effective and efficient problem-solving method.

KEYS TO SUCCESSFUL PROBLEM SOLVING

1. *Stay objective*. Suppose Ed, one of your customer representatives, just slammed the phone down after speaking with an irate user. Now is the time to talk to him. As you approach him, be ready to deal with Ed in a diplomatic way. If you dash into the situation with guns blazing, Ed's ears are going to close down and the two of you probably won't get anywhere. Instead, when talking with him, describe the situation in objective terms. Speak about what he did or didn't do. Don't call him names or guess his motivation. Outline the problem in a concise, accurate way. For example, you might say, "Ed, you just slammed the phone down pretty hard just now." This definitely beats out, "Ed, you nitwit. What the heck makes you think it's okay to slam the phone down? You're always so quick to do stupid things when you're upset." By using the first approach, you have a good start toward keeping Ed's mind open and helping him deal with the situation in a rational way.

The second response will automatically produce defensive behavior. Ed won't get too excited about solving this problem, and you've gotten nowhere.

2. *Determine what happened*. Ask Ed what happened. Don't ask him while shouting or making an accusation. It's in your best problem-solving interest to find out what caused Ed to respond in this way. His explanation might be that the individual on the other end swore at him and took ten minutes to tell Ed how he was going to get him fired because he couldn't solve the problem on the spot. That was the sixth similar phone call Ed had fielded that morning, and he just lost it for a minute. On the other hand, Ed might reply, "They had it coming. I'm sick and tired of babying these people." The answer will alert you to the best approach to resolving the issue.

3. *Ask for suggestions*. Now, you may have had this experience when you were in Ed's shoes a few years ago. At that time you came up with a surefire solution to the problem. You could leap in with your suggestion, without asking Ed's opinion first. After all, you solved the problem ten years ago by making yourself count to ten and rubbing your temples, then shooting a few wastepaper baskets until the pain went away. You may believe you're doing Ed a favor in coming up with a solution so fast. That way he won't have to put any effort into it and his problem will be quickly solved. But the problem with someone else's idea is exactly that. It is someone else's idea. We always like our own ideas better than someone else's, because they are custom-made to suit our particular needs. The reason your solution worked so well for you is that you came up with it. Let Ed have the same privilege.

Discipline yourself. Instead of leaping in with your terrific suggestion, ask Ed what he might do differently next time he is faced with that situation. You are steps ahead in the game when you do this. Ed's confidence will build because you're smart enough to ask his opinion; his loyalty to you will grow as well. He also is required to think the situation through, and the answers he comes up with will more likely be ones he can implement.

Ed may suggest that the next time he feels he's going to lose his cool, he should squeeze the racquetball he keeps in the top drawer of his desk. Then, after he gets off the phone, he should get up, go for a drink of water or coffee, and take a spin down the corridor. Don't "yes, but" him. More good ideas have been squelched with the words, "yes, but" than by any other phrase. Most managers believe this is a way of verifying what an individual says and then adding their own thoughts.

However, when the word *but* enters any conversation, in actuality it means, "Forget it."

Some managers think they offer an opportunity for input when, after making their suggestion, they then ask employees if they have any ideas. Usually employees mumble no and shake their head. Why? In their mind, it would be a waste of time to come up with any other ideas. You're the boss and basically you have told them how to deal with the situation in a way that is to your satisfaction. When you speak first, it's a bright signal that says you've made up your mind. Your request for suggestions appears to the employee as an afterthought. Very few people will stick their neck out to counteract what the boss has already said. More likely you'll hear, "Yeah, that's a good idea, I'll give it a try." When employees do give it a try, however, it may not be their ticket for a successful solution.

4. *Use employee suggestions.* If at all possible, use suggestions offered by your employees. You may well believe you have a better one, but keep your goal in mind. You want to encourage risk taking as well as solve problems. If every time they offer a suggestion you shoot it down with one of your own, it will be a very short time before employees quit trying to come up with ideas. Together, you are trying to solve problems. The path employees choose to reach that goal may be different from the one you would select; however, if their method solves the problem, let them try it their way.

If you note a major flaw in their suggestion, help them see the problem with such questions as, "If you do that, what do you think might happen?" Work together to envision the possible results if their plan is put into action. Share some standards for what you consider a good plan. If, for example, Ed had decided that a good solution would be to put the phone down gently, then scream an ancient curse, you'd want to let him know that you expected a quieter solution. Then, encourage him to come up with another idea.

5. *Insist that employees contribute their suggestions.* When you try to get people involved in problem solving, keep in mind that you are not managing new people; you always are working with "used" employees. These people have had a variety of experiences involving problem solving with a manager. Perhaps they were never asked for their opinions on the job, so their brain cells have gotten flabby and they need some exercise to get them in shape again. A second possibility is that they may have been ridiculed, "yes-butted," or their suggestions discounted when they attempted to participate in the process. They

may now assume the defense of "I don't know" or "I can't think of anything" to protect themselves.

If your employees respond with shuffling feet, averted eyes, and a mumbled, "I don't know," let them know that you really want their help. Make them believe this is the case by not answering your own question, even if the silence gets uncomfortable. After the quiet time passes from reasonable thinking time to dead air, say something like, "I'd really value your suggestions since you live the problem every day and I don't. How about if you think about it overnight and we get back together tomorrow at 2:00 and discuss it?"

Generally two things happen. Employees are both amazed and dismayed that you don't jump in with a solution. They are amazed because most managers leap at the opportunity to strut their cleverness. They are dismayed because now they have to come up with a solution. Not only are they responsible for coming up with a plan, but they are concerned about your reaction to their idea and what might possibly happen as a result. Remember, this sort of experience hasn't worked well for them in the past. The next day, meet at 2:00, listen to their idea, and implement it if at all possible. Building power muscles by giving people a chance to use them is what this activity is all about. After they flex these muscles a bit, and learn what your standards are for usable solutions, they will start coming up with answers independently. This is the way you get people solving problems on their own. Initially it takes time, but over the long haul the return on your investment is significant.

6. *Agree on the plan.* Ask your employees what they will do that will be different next time. "I'll try harder" is not an acceptable answer. When employees make choices, they select the option they see as best at the time. Your job as coach is to help them see other alternatives. When they can get away with "I'll try harder," they haven't given the thought to the situation that can turn it around. Pin them down to specifics: what are they going to do differently and when are they going to make that change?

7. *Follow up on the results.* After employees have had time to put a solution in place, follow up to see how it's going. Many managers scoff at this idea. Their reasoning is that when employees solve the problem, they are doing their jobs the way they should have been doing them in the first place. In their minds, that doesn't call for special recognition. But smart management believes that it does. You want to follow up to make sure things are going the way you want them to go. If they are

not, you need further problem solving. But if they are, it's a smart idea to reinforce the change.

When employees put forth the effort to solve a problem, they are changing their behaviors and maybe even their habits. This is not an easy thing to do. Help them. By noticing that the problem has been resolved through their own efforts, you help them keep that change in place. If you don't take the time to follow up and see that their efforts are paying off, you send a message I bet you don't want to send. Without follow-up, employees reason that you probably don't care whether the situation changes or not. Since they have much on the job to put their energies toward, they'll choose something that seems a higher priority. Then, you have the discouraging experience of believing the problem is resolved but then witnessing that they are continuing with the previous behavior. Without follow-up, this result is guaranteed.

The follow-up doesn't have to be elaborate. Just notice and say something to the effect of, "I see you're working on changing [whatever the employee is working on]; I appreciate the effort. Keep up the good work." Change doesn't happen in quantum leaps. It starts small and grows as employees get used to operating differently. Help them to make the complete change by recognizing their efforts along the way.

AVOID THREE COMMON
MOTIVATIONAL MISTAKES

It's easy to involve your staff in problem solving when you can peg the problem. There are times, though, that you can't figure out what's going on. You are putting into action all the best management techniques you know how to use, yet you are puzzled and discouraged by the reactions of your staff. You feel you're encouraging your people, involving them in problem solving, giving them feedback, and overall, displaying confidence in their abilities. Yet at times you feel so confused. Employees take action that either goes directly against what you have requested or seems to act against their own best interests. This dilemma makes you question your own motivation as well. Let's look at some typical examples.

☐ Ned is a lawyer with a small firm that manufactures safety equipment. He's an all-around good ace, a real team member who contributes at a high level. He's intelligent and competent at what he does. Mark, his manager, can't figure out why lately Ned insists on telling people who request his services that he must check with Mark before making a commitment. Mark has told Ned many times that he trusts his judgment. Ned's always worked independently, and Mark has encouraged that. This sudden shift in behavior has got Mark stumped.

☐ Bud is an analyst with a publishing firm. Sue, his manager, has repeatedly asked him not to jerryrig the computer equipment because the department is housed in an old building and when he does, it sometimes causes a power surge and then he can't use his terminal for a while. It's gotten so serious, in fact, that the last time Bud did this, Sue reprimanded him and even told him that if it happened again, a disciplinary letter would be put in his file. She doesn't want to take that action because Bud is such a good worker otherwise, but she can't have him molesting the equipment. Sue knows her approval means a lot to Bud and he really wants to advance with this company. These black marks aren't going to help his chances for promotion.

☐ Roger, head of personnel for a real-estate management group, is scratching his head at the lack of response from his staff. He requested that they submit monthly summaries of their activities so he can stay on top of what's going on and can have a full, written set of data at performance-review time. He isn't asking for anything special, nor particularly time consuming. He just wants a brief, handwritten page or two. This won't take his employees more than fifteen minutes to complete, yet no one gets the report in on time. Some of them don't turn them in at all. Roger has made a real effort to make this an easy expectation, yet no one is meeting it.

Odd as their reactions may seem, these employees are responding to their situations in a reasonable manner. People avoid what hurts and strive for what feels good. It's only common sense. The problem is that managers all have their blind sides when it comes to determining what hurts or feels good for other people. Most managers tend to make judgments based on their own preferences.

Three common mistakes managers make are to (1) penalize someone for good performance, (2) reward someone for poor or nonperformance, and (3) give employees the message that their performance doesn't matter. You might wonder what foolish manager would make these mistakes. Actually, every manager probably has at one time or another. To increase your problem-solving success with employees, it's an excellent idea to keep these three common errors in mind.

Mark, Sue, and Roger are managers making the usual mistake of analyzing what is going on with their employees from their own points of view, not from the employees'. This has tremendous potential to cripple the very action orientation they want their employees to have. Let's jump into the employees' shoes for a minute and consider these situations from their view.

Doing What You Want Them to Do Hurts Them

In the case of Ned, who isn't making a move without Mark's approval, you need to know that the last time Ned accepted an assignment without checking with Mark, he lost an opportunity that was important to him. He was working diligently at a special request from Herb, a peer of Mark's, when Mark appeared on the scene. Mark took a look at what Ned was doing and commented in front of the rest of the staff, "Well, it's certainly your choice if you want to do that project for Herb. Since you're busy with his job, I guess I'll have to give the VP's project to Joan. Too bad you don't have time. I'd have liked to see you shine on this one."

There's little wonder why Ned keeps running to Mark. He figures that Mark has information he doesn't have, and he might miss an opportunity again if he makes decisions on projects without Mark's input or approval. Ned feels he looked like not only a poor decision maker but an outright fool in front of his coworkers. Mark didn't mean any harm; in fact, he believes he was reinforcing Ned's independence. In addition, Mark believes he was endorsing his belief in Ned's ability by telling him he had intended him for the vice president's project. In reality, Ned feels he is being punished for working independently.

Not Doing What You Want Has Positive Results

Bud uses the computer quite creatively. Why? When his equipment is unusable, Sue gives him special projects instead. Her reasoning is that these projects have to be done, and she can't do them all. Bud does a good job on them and Sue doesn't want his down time to be unproductive. Bud loves these special projects. They're a lot more fun than much of his routine work assignments.

People outside of Bud's department see his work on these special projects; they don't see his routine work. They notice how competent he is with the results he produces on these specials. They tell Bud how impressed they are with the work he does. In fact, the promotion pot is beginning to boil, heated by his special-project work. Sue's dilemma is that the only time Bud gets to work on these special projects is when his equipment is down. Sue's not getting the performance she expects because there are greater rewards for Bud when he doesn't do what he's supposed to, rather than when he does. When Bud does what Sue objects to, he gets work he enjoys more, with higher visibility and greater possibilities for promotion. Sue hasn't provided these rewards in Bud's daily routine, so he has had to create them himself.

Doing What You Want Doesn't Matter

How about Roger's late—or altogether missing—summaries? Roger does nothing when the reports are submitted or when they're not. He does nothing if they're on time or late. From his employees' point of view, why should they waste their time? They have duties and deadlines that matter and for which there is a consequence. These summaries don't appear to be a priority for Roger, so they feel it would be foolish to invest their time in a "no-matter" situation.

FOUR QUESTIONS TO FIX THE PROBLEM

Analyze the employee behavior that may be puzzling you. Do problem employees receive something "good," such as power, visibility, time off, or attention, when they don't do what they're supposed to, as in Bud's case? Or does something "bad" or painful happen as a result of honoring your request, as in Ned's case? Does it seem to matter whether someone performs as you ask? This analysis is difficult because so few managers can see the forest for the trees.

You're in the thick of things, invested in your actions, and you have difficulty stepping back to assess the situation. If you are puzzled by the behavior of your employees, ask yourself a few questions. Put the answers down in writing. Writing forces you to be more specific, keeping you from just muddling the answers around in your head.

1. What specifically do you want them to do?
2. What are they doing now?
3. What happens to them when they do this?
4. What happens to them when they do what you want them to?

(Make sure to look at this answer from their point of view, not yours.)

Once you have answered these questions, you have some guidelines for turning the situation around.

CHANGE THE CONSEQUENCES

To change Ned's behavior back to working more independently, Mark had a conversation with Ned. Together they worked out a communication plan so that Ned won't be caught out in the cold again. To change Bud's behavior, Sue arranged to have him work on special projects on a regular basis. She added a little insurance to the pot by letting Bud know that if he jerryrigged the equipment again, he wouldn't receive any more special projects. Bud's behavior changed immediately.

Roger turned his situation around by posting a calendar outside his door. He listed the names of staff members who were to submit their monthly summaries. When they got their reports in on time, he pasted gold stars next to their names. When the reports were late but turned in within two weeks, they got red stars. When they were missing in action by the week following the due date, black stars were placed next to their names. Did this have an effect? You bet it did. Ridiculous as it sounds, it was a great motivator. After three months, the majority of stars were gold. What Roger accomplished by this seemingly silly way of dealing with the problem was to let his people know that he did, in fact, notice and care if the reports were turned in. The list lent a lighter touch to the message because it turned the problem into an office joke.

YOU TRY SOME

Case 1

Everyone comes late for staff meeting. Craig has told them it's important to get there when expected for efficient use of that expensive meeting time. Yet everyone is late. Jason comes in as much as half an hour late each time. He's out of breath from rushing and always has a good excuse, but Craig can set his watch by him. Pretend you're Craig and analyze the situation.

1. What do you want the staff to do?
2. What are they doing now?
3. What happens when they do what they do? Is it good or bad?
4. What happens when they do what you want—that is, come to meetings on time? Is it good or bad in their opinion?
5. What could you do to turn the situation around?

Case 2

As a reward for great teamwork on a project, Lisa arranges that her employees present their results to the department heads instead of making the presentation herself. The presentation is one week away and they still can't come to closure even on their outline, though they've been working steadily for days. Pretend you're Lisa and ask yourself the key questions.

Case 3

The file clerks in a hospital information department don't file single-sheet lab reports in the patient records. They know it's important and they realize that the record is not complete without these sheets, yet the reports sit for weeks in the basket, not being filed. The hospital is losing money. You're their supervisor. Ask the questions and make a recommendation.

The Case of the Meeting Mystery

Craig sets the meeting time for 10:00 A.M. Since everyone isn't there and he hates to repeat himself, he waits until about 10:10 or 10:15 to start. He wants the staff to be there on time and to get all the information. What happens when they do what they want to do? They don't waste that ten or fifteen minutes Craig spends waiting for others to arrive. Jason, the latecomer, has a great need for attention and power.

When he arrives late, he meets some of those needs. First, he interrupts the meeting. Second, as Craig goes over all the information that had been covered earlier, Jason gets a feeling of importance because Craig has imposed on everyone else's time to fill Jason in.

The solution? Craig starts the meetings on time and doesn't repeat information for latecomers. He makes it their responsibility to get their hands on the minutes or to meet with someone who was there. He doesn't pay special attention to Jason when he arrives. The results? People started coming on time, Jason included.

The Case of the Reluctant Presenters

What does Lisa want her staff to do? She wants them to make a presentation that will highlight their work to some influential people. What are they doing now? Procrastinating so that the work won't be the best they can produce. Lisa is concerned that they will not do themselves justice. What will happen if they do what Lisa wants? They will become highly visible. They are frightened of that much visibility all at once. Instead of being viewed as a reward, her staff sees this assignment as painful. These employees have never made a presentation before to such an important group and they don't feel capable or confident. They are afraid that their chances for advancement will be hindered by making this presentation.

The solution? Lisa finds out about their concerns. She coaches them in presentation skills, fills them in on the things that this particular group likes to see in presentations. She helps them develop their content and gives them some money to produce very nice slides. The result? They quit procrastinating and produce a nice program. They do quite well and are very proud of themselves.

The Case of the Unfiled Lab Reports

The clerks aren't filing single-sheet reports. What happens when they do? Nothing. What happens when they don't? Nothing.

The solution? The supervisor sets up a reward system of ten extra break minutes for every twenty-five lab slips filed. She creates an easy tracking system. The slips are now up to date, records are complete, and the hospital is no longer losing money.

The habit of analyzing situations for the secret payoffs or punishments can be an extremely valuable one. Clouds can clear away when you look at puzzling situations from this perspective. If you're having a tough time figuring out a problem, enlist the help of a trusted peer or friend. Sometimes that third ear or eye is able to hear or see things that zip by you.

With both good analysis and manager-employee partnership in problem solving, you're well on your way to creating a climate that encourages action and promotes getting things done. You'll have a staff of committed employees who are able to solve problems independently and to your satisfaction.

Chapter 6

Getting People to Change

There is nothing as stable as change. And there is no job more frustrating, maddening, or downright confusing than trying to manage the changes that go on every day. Some people thrive on change. Most don't, and the latter group probably makes up the majority of your staff. Since change is an everyday part of life, a large aspect of your job as manager is to implement change successfully. Sounds easy, right? How're you doing?

☐ The coffeepot sits on a shelf over a jutting ledge. People chance injury simply by pouring themselves a cup of coffee. One evening you decide to move the pot before you leave the office, and you put it around the corner in a less hazardous spot. The reaction? People can't stop complaining about how inconvenient it is to go all the way around the corner to get a simple cup of coffee.

☐ You have fought for bigger, more comfortable space for your staff.

After a long battle, you've won, and you announce at a staff meeting that in two weeks they can move to more spacious, air-conditioned quarters. The reaction? People are up in arms, not believing you'd do this to them. They complain that the new space is inconvenient, that the parking won't be as good, and that this is the absolute busiest time of the year. There isn't time to pack and move. How could you be so inconsiderate?

☐ Your staff has complained for several months that the time-keeping system is burdensome and time consuming as well as from the dark ages. You arrange with Information Systems to design a computerized time keeping system that will be less difficult and speedier. The reaction? Disbelief that you would do this to them. How can you expect them to add one more job to their schedules.

What's going on? Are these people just complainers by nature? Are they merely a bunch of ingrates? Or are they experiencing a normal reaction to change? Unfortunately, this is typical behavior when people are confronted with change.

RESISTING CHANGE

Most of us fight change whether the change is "good" or "bad." Employees don't resist change just because they want to make your life miserable or difficult, or because they are unreasonable or cranky. People fight new things for two reasons. First, the experience of change is not particularly pleasant, even if the change is a positive one. Second, they are concerned or fearful of the possible results of the change. Change, by definition, is doing something different. In doing something difficult, they must face the unknown, whereas life before change is predictable and comfortable.

People work out ways of coping, and because of this, they feel capable and competent and achieving. They know how and where to find information. They know who to go to for problem solving. They know how to fix the stuck doors with a ruler and when to count on a power surge so they can turn off the computers. They have learned the quirks of the persons they work with. For instance, they know that when John wears his red tie, they shouldn't talk to him. When Susan says, "I'm a little upset," it means a blowout is coming, so batten down the hatches. They choose the times when Ken pulls out his pipe to ask him for something. In other words, they can count on their world and deal effectively with it.

When change happens, the familiar goes up in smoke. All the things they counted on no longer work. People don't feel capable or confident anymore. Change takes a lot of energy as well, and most people fight having to put in the energy it takes to change. Because change causes loss of confidence, it interferes with the action orientation you'd like your staff to have. People take more action when they have confidence in the results and feel sure of their part in those results. Therefore, it's in your best interest to understand the process of change so that you can help people feel more comfortable when it happens. This way they are willing to make changes more often.

EXPERIENCING THE CHANGE

The processes that people experience during change are a bit different, depending on whether it is a negative or a positive change. But there are more similarities than differences. When going through any change, people start out ignoring the change itself or even the chance of change. Most hope that the ostrich approach of burying their heads in the sand will make the change go away. Even if you had told your people for six months in advance that you were trying to get them better quarters, they still would act as if it were the world's biggest surprise when they heard the news. Each time you mentioned the upcoming change during the previous six months, they would probably have made comments such as, "We've heard that before," "He'll never be able to pull it off." For some people, it won't sink in until the packing cartons arrive from the movers.

After they wrestle with the impending change for a while, most people accept the fact and realize that the change is, in fact, going to take place whether they like it or not. When that happens, people find themselves wavering between anger and depression. This is not a particularly tidy process, unfortunately. Anger can and does sneak up on people, just as depression can and often does. People never quite know which emotion is going to hit or for how long. They usually feel very confused. This is particularly puzzling when the change is a "good" one, as in the case of this office move.

Hearts Follow Heads

By the time people are on their way to experiencing anger and depression, they have decided intellectually that the change is all right and that they will certainly be able to cope. In the case of the office move, on paper it looks terrific. The new offices are bigger, they are in a better section of town, there is air-conditioning, and it's right near the best deli within 100 miles. The staff will keep exclaiming, "What's not to like?" when they start discussing the move. But most of them are having a tough time shaking free of depression, or they are finding themselves snapping at others for hardly any reason. There's that darned headache that won't go away and the knot in their stomach feels like a permanent fixture.

In their minds, the staff believe they are feeling positive about the move, yet their emotional reactions seem out of whack. This is a very confusing and uncomfortable experience. People usually try to shake themselves out of this phase with pep talks. Another favorite is lecturing themselves and others, particularly when they feel irritable. Most people don't know enough about the process of change to make the connection between these awful feelings and the change itself. They keep fighting the reaction when the smartest thing to do is ride it out. Fighting the anger, depression, and frustration only extends them and makes people feel worse.

In spite of it all, people survive these confusing, tough times and proceed with the change. As they go through the changes, they test themselves and give the change a chance. They begin to feel more comfortable with the difference and start finding ways to make the change work for them. After a while, people get so used to the new way that if you were to suggest they go back to the old way, they would fight you just as hard as they did in the first place. What's going on? Why do people experience these emotions when going through change?

The Change Cycle

Remember, *change* is defined as something different. When we move from one thing to another, whether it's our own idea or someone else's, we are losing something. In the case of the office move, yes, many things were being gained, but many things were being lost. In the old office, friends were left. Routes to work had to be changed and people couldn't operate on automatic pilot for a while. The warmth of being greeted by Ralph, the security man, was left behind. The cookie shop next door became a thing of the past. All these things may sound small and petty, but they make up the fabric of everyday life. When you cut that fabric, holes are left and it takes some time to weave it whole again. All too often, people discount these little things that contribute to a feeling of security and confidence.

Thus, human beings have predictable ways of dealing with loss or change. They get shaken from their stable position and go into a period of shock and then denial. They experience strong feelings of anger and depression. Next, comes the testing period for the new way, and finally, the adjustment is made. This is never a particularly pleasant experience, and since we go through it every time we experience change, we have a natural tendency to avoid change. Fighting change seems pretty sensible when you think about it.

Positive Change

It's puzzling that people have the same painful reaction when the change is a happy or positive one right from the start. For example, Sharon was promoted to manager of the human resources section in which she had been working for a considerable time. She could not understand why, after achieving a goal she had sought for so long, she felt so sad and angry. When she realized that she was reacting to her losses, it was at least more understandable, if not more comfortable. What had Sharon lost? Her place in the group. Her office space, which she had arranged for her convenience. Her custom of grousing about the boss with her coworkers. Sharon also lost the easy feeling of competence she had on her previous job. It is hoped she'll regain those things with her new position, but in the meantime she's very uncomfortable.

Changes we look forward to not only entail dealing with the regular losses but involve one more loss that is part of the changes we welcome. When we head toward a good change, hopes are high. People are confident that the new way will be worth the energy it takes to pull it off. After a while, reality sets in. Everything isn't as rosy as hoped. So, the additional loss to be dealt with is that of the optimism that always accompanies the beginning of a positive change.

The good news is that after coping with the disillusionment, a second reality sets in: realistic optimism. As people progress through positive change, they grow more confident and work with the change until they reach a satisfied state.

FIGHTING THE FEAR

Besides wanting to avoid the unpleasant experience of change, people fight or avoid what's new because they aren't sure what the results will mean for them. Fear is the overriding emotion when it comes to change. Fear of what? Fear of the unknown. The unknown stirs up concern over whether we'll be a success or a failure. We're afraid what people will think and how they will react. There are lots of fears lurking in the background that often are never identified or addressed.

Fear of Failing

The most common fear when change is discussed is that of failure. People are afraid they won't be as good at the new as they were at the old. This is predictable, since as individuals go through change they must learn something new. When a transcription pool switched from typewriters to word processors, production went down dramatically. In learning the new system, workers found that the old tricks of the trade no longer worked. They were not yet familiar with the new machinery, so they hadn't yet come up with new tricks to make themselves as efficient. It's a normal part of what is called the learning curve, namely, that people aren't as good at something new as they are at something familiar.

Lack of confidence is an unsettling feeling, and there is always the concern that individuals will never again be as proficient as they once were. That conjures up all sorts of fears. Workers are afraid that they might lose their jobs. They are worried that they will lose the respect of their manager, and that of their coworkers. The desire to achieve and feel powerful is a top motivating force. When experiencing change, people don't achieve and they don't feel powerful. It's not a pleasant experience, and people are afraid they are going to look foolish and possibly be ridiculed.

Fear of Succeeding

The fear that is a little more surprising is that of success. It certainly seems that if individuals are so concerned about failing, success would be a welcome relief. Surprisingly, it houses just as many goblins. One reason people are afraid of success is that they worry that if they are too successful, they may be asked to take on even more and they're not sure they can handle the extra load. A lot of people are afraid of success because they think it will set a pattern of expectation they can't match. They feel that if they are too good at adjusting to change people will come to expect it of them.

Another reason people shy away from success is concern about what others think of them. If they are too good, will they still be part of the group or will they turn into outsiders? Will people think they are snobs, trying to win the boss's favor or just showing off?

People are often afraid of whether success will change them personally. Everyone envisions a picture of a "successful person," whether conscious or not. Tom, a supervisor in one of my workshops, had lots of money come to mind along with a real sense of anxiety when he pictured what success meant to him. His anxiety about success and the money he believed went with it triggered a feeling deep down that he wouldn't handle the money well. Susan, another member of that workshop, panicked when she pictured what success was to her, because she believed it meant you were never allowed to make a mistake again. Aaron realized that subconsciously he believed success in his company meant an overseas assignment, which was something he didn't want because he had other important obligations.

Another factor in the fear of success is the sense of an inability on our part to live up to the outward change. Sharon put it so well when she said, "You may be promoted outwardly, but inwardly you're not promoted." She feared success because she wasn't sure she could live up to the expectations of the promotion. Fear of success sometimes leads to a feeling of dishonesty. Sharon claimed that if she accepted that promotion, it would be a public declaration that she believed she could do the job. She felt this was dishonest because she was quaking in her boots and was worried she'd be found out.

Fear of Conflict

People are often afraid that a change might bring about conflict with others as well as conflict within themselves. One of the workers in the transcription pool confided that she was afraid to make the change because if she were successful, other transcriptionists might label her a "goody-goody" and make her life miserable. She didn't want to chance facing any of the conflicts that might be involved. The bottom-line fear is, "Can I cope?" "What conflicts will appear?" "Can I handle them?" "Can I handle myself?"

WHY ATTEMPTS TO IMPLEMENT CHANGE OFTEN FAIL

Many managers hesitate to explore fear of change and to consider what the change will mean with their staff members. This may be because they are concerned about the change as well and may be experiencing many of the same fears. Additional anxiety often comes because managers think they can't address the concerns of the staff without dumping the plans for the change. Usually employee concerns are reasonable ones; their real needs probably don't involve anything that drastic. If you don't address their concerns, they grow out of proportion and the change is even more difficult to institute. The very act of talking about the change reduces fear and resistance. By acknowledging their concerns and anxieties as legitimate, you remove one of the greatest barriers to change. By not only allowing but actually helping your staff to work through these issues, you demonstrate that this is a team effort and that their comfort and security are important to you.

Managers often think they are responsible for coming up with all the answers for the concerns that are voiced. Instead, share that responsibility with your staff. They probably have some excellent thoughts on how to deal with these issues. Often, your job just to provide some guidance or the resources to implement the solutions. Sometimes, your job consists solely of listening. People frequently just need a concerned and sympathetic ear.

By dealing with these concerns up front, you offer a buy-in for your staff. If you wait, they eventually adjust to the change, but a lot of negative feelings are created unnecessarily, which interfere with successful timing and maybe full implementation. Avoiding the issues likewise has another side effect: it can make it much more difficult to implement change the next time.

If your staff is partner in the change process, your employees feel they have some control. This empowerment makes them more action prone and willing to try. The next time you want to implement change, you are steps ahead in the game because you arranged a success experience for them during the previous change. There is no negative residue and people are more enthusiastic and confident about the change than they normally would be.

OVERCOMING RESISTANCE TO CHANGE

There are a few additional actions you can take to boost people over the hurdles they encounter when making changes and taking action. Most fears, whether of success, failure, personal change, or potential conflict, center on being able to cope effectively with the unknown. Smart managers help make that fearful unknown more familiar right from the start. They work to make their people feel powerful and confident about the change, by fostering these feelings in a variety of ways.

Tell Them About the Process

One of the first things smart managers do is inform people about the process of change. Let your staff know why it's normal to resist change and why people feel uncomfortable going through change. Tell them that the process does end comfortably, and they will soon fight going back to the old way just as hard as they fight the new. Find some examples to send that point home. For example, one group understood that point very well when it was good-naturedly pointed out to them that, when they were asked to change parking structures involving only going around a corner, everyone was up in arms. Then two years later, when they were asked to go back to parking in the original structure, they had just as many arguments and complaints.

People feel relieved when they hear that what they are experiencing is normal. Even though the reaction to change is still uncomfortable, it's easier to handle when people know what is going on. Help them realize it's normal to feel anxious, even about positive change. Fill people in on what they can expect, and they will feel much freer to discuss the whole process with you. By discussing the aspects of change in an open atmosphere, you open up avenues for honest communication that lead to smooth implementation of change. By being made aware of the process of change, your employees can help identify what needs to be done, not only for themselves but also for others, to ensure a smooth change.

Involve Them in Planning

It's common sense for people to resist someone else's idea until they can see how it's going to fit into their lives. You can help achieve positive fit by involving your employees in planning for the change as soon as you can. Right from the start, this can be involvement in what the change will be. For example, this would have been appropriate in the incident with the office coffeepot. I'm not suggesting a major task force to decide on moving the coffeepot, but it would have been smart to devote five minutes at a staff meeting to the topic.

It may be that a change simply must happen, and your staff won't have the luxury of a say in the matter. Possibly, a change has been decreed by top management. Another instance is when a change must happen because the present way of operating is not as productive as it could be. As soon as you can, get your people involved in planning to implement that change. For example, to make the switch from the old, handwritten time-keeping system, Sally, the manager, asked her staff what they wanted from the new system. She explored what would be useful and what were their concerns. She had the group meet with the Information Systems consultant so that their concerns and ideas were passed on firsthand. The result was a workable system better than anything Sally or the consultant could have created, thanks to the input of the potential users. The best part was that implementation of the change was smooth, and the new system was useful, accepted right from the start.

Weaken the Barriers

To help people work through a change, whether as individuals or as a staff group, encourage them to think about their issues and fears. Have them consider the positive aspects of the change, too. Every change has forces that push people to go along with it, and every change has forces that keep people from making the transition. Work with your people to figure out what these are. After you have identified them, come up with a plan to strengthen the positive forces and weaken the negative ones. For instance, the transcriptionists switching to the word-processing system came up with the following list. (Keep in mind that they worked on an incentive-pay system, which meant that the faster they produced, the more money they earned.)

FOR	AGAINST
Eventually faster	Slower in the beginning, so lose money
Can keep date	
Can make changes faster	Don't know if I can do it
Can make more money, maybe	Am afraid of computers
Can upgrade the equipment for even more money	Have heard staring at CRT is damaging to health
Quieter	
Don't have to worry about spelling	They're going to make us do it before we're ready

After the transcriptionists pegged the forces that were part of the change, the manager and employees set about to strengthen the factors that helped the change and to weaken the ones that discouraged it. One solution was that the manager created an intermediate incentive system. For the first few months, during which it would take time to get used to the system and build speed on the new machines, the workers wouldn't lose money. This provided a less threatening atmosphere for them to find out if they could do it or not; the grace period allowed time for their confidence to rebuild.

To address the issue of computer fear, the manager invited three people from another area who used this equipment in their work every day to a staff meeting. These people answered questions about day-to-day workings, and after this discussion, many of the transcriptionists' fears were put to rest. Also, two of the typists were given work time to research information on the health hazards of working with CRTs. Management worked with the staff on implementing a time frame, so that the staff didn't feel pushed when the equipment was in and ready to use.

One note of caution about timing. Give people time to get used to the idea of a change. Rushing through a change can spell disaster. One thing to remember is that, as manager, you are about ten steps ahead of your employees in adjusting to the change, simply because you probably have known about it longer. That's easy to forget, however. The result is that when you feel comfortable with the change, you assume your employees feel the same. Chances are they don't, so give them time to catch up, if at all possible.

By including the staff in planning the change, you certainly don't remove all reluctance. However, if you reduce the scarier factors of the change and weaken some of the barriers, the change goes much more smoothly and successfully.

Make It Fit

Many times, people resist change because they believe the change will interfere with reaching some other goals that are important to them. For example, Jim was upset when his company formed a speaker's bureau and his name was put on the list because of his experiences overseas. His concern was that many of the speaking engagements were at night or out of town. He and his wife had just adopted twins, a dream they had waited years to come true. He saw this speaker's bureau as interfering with his enjoyment and participation in a long-awaited goal.

Jim's manager, Maxine, was a smart individual when it came to implementing change, and she worked with him right from the start. Jim was the type of worker who would go ahead and do what the company requested in spite of his own needs. On the surface, he'd be pretty cheery about it. Maxine had noticed in the past that Jim was supportive, even enthusiastic, about some changes that were not particularly convenient for him, but he had a tendency to start missing deadlines as those changes were implemented. He also would forget key steps in the process. She figured out that this was Jim's way of protesting the changes. Jim didn't want to take the chance of resisting outwardly, so he resisted in subconscious ways.

This is not unusual. The normal reaction to change is initial resistance, even if it's just a fleeting thought. People who don't acknowledge that resistance express it anyway, whether they are aware of it or not. Maxine decided to deal with the problem—or in this case, potential problem—up front. Together they examined the positives in this situation and looked at Jim's concerns. The only real drawback to the change was Jim's desire to spend time with the twins. To settle the issue before it ever came up, Jim and Maxine negotiated with the speaker's bureau management to never book Jim for more than one speaking engagement per week after 6 P.M. and not more than two out-of-town per month. This was an excellent move because Jim was a very talented and popular speaker once he got started. He could have been swamped with invitations, with no avenue for protest. But this way, he not only supported the change but became enthusiastic about it. Ahead of time, the major threat of the change was eliminated.

Create New Rewards

Expect resistance when people's habits will be affected. In a previous example, everyone was used to walking to work in their usual morning fog, grabbing their coffee cup, and going on automatic pilot to the coffeepot. Why should there be such an uproar about moving the pot around the corner? People had to change a habit. Something that didn't require any thought now took some thought and some energy. Most individuals are efficient. Habits are established and patterns are formed because they work; people don't have to invest thought each time they do the same action. It's a pretty good way to operate, until change is introduced. So, people will resist and complain until they establish a new habit pattern that works just as well as the old one did.

Since there's a loss with every change, try to have the price match the reward. If employees see that they will have to give up some very important things and they will have very little to show for it, of course they will resist the change. Work with them to find out what returns they need to make the change worthwhile for them. Then, if possible, do whatever you can to have the two match. In the case of the coffeepot, eventually the reward of not getting jabbed was a great payoff for having a habit upset.

KEEP ON TOP OF INFORMATION

Communicate as much information as you can about the impending change. Explain the purpose and need for the switch. People like to be included in a change, and if a change has to happen over which you or they have little control, at least tell them why someone else decided this would be a good idea.

Try, in as many ways as you can think of, to make the unfamiliar familiar. If you are moving, take the staff to the new site to look around and get comfortable with it. If you are installing new equipment, arrange time for people to play with it; get training for them, provide instructional manuals. If a new process is being put in place, find out as much as you can about it and pass that information on to your staff. These actions convey the message that you and your staff truly are partners in change.

ENSURE ACCURATE INFORMATION

People on the receiving end often take the news of a change and twist it around to suit their expectations or hopes. To make sure people don't get done in by this kind of behavior, keep the lines of communication clear and open. Check the grapevine to see what gossip is being spread. If the rumors don't resemble reality, call the group together to talk about the differences between the official information and what these people are hearing.

Inaccuracies can alert you to possible issues and concerns. For example, people were fighting tooth and nail against having air-conditioning put into an older building. The official communiqué said that new windows would be put in to make the air-conditioning efficient. When the manager explored why people were fighting the change, he found a rumor going around that the windows would be sealed shut. The situation was corrected by passing on the "real" information. The windows would be locked, not sealed, and the keys were not going to be in the hands of some invisible, inflexible facility manager. Each group would have the key to operate the locks on its windows so as to have some control over its situation. The fears had grown way out of proportion because the idea of control was an extremely important issue for many employees.

In summary, by taking the time and putting in the energy to create opportunities for your employees to be partners in change, you'll increase their action orientation. By knowing what to expect from the change cycle, they can predict their reactions and be ready for the problems. Then you and your staff can put plans in place to cope effectively with both the cycle and the results of change. Frustration and confusion are reduced. Employees feel much more in control, which increases self-esteem and the probability for success. Success promotes success, and success promotes action.

Chapter 7

Pave the Road to Action

People take action when they believe they will be successful. Your job as manager is to lay the foundation for a can-do team by boosting your employees' confidence and self-esteem. People who feel good about themselves are willing to try new ideas and act much more readily.

MANAGEMENT PLUS EXCEPTION

One way to increase self-esteem is to make sure positive feedback reaches your employees. Most managers work on the principle of "management by exception." This basically means that they keep their eyes open to spot problems. To create an action atmosphere with your team, try using "management *plus* exception." With this method, you are still alert to problems, but also pay attention to things going smoothly. The greatest motivator is a sense of achievement, as proved by studies done over the past twenty-five years. Right in line behind this is recognition of achievement. Management plus exception opens your eyes to accomplishments so you can arrange for recognition.

Management plus exception is easily implemented. For example, Cynthia was the head nurse of a large division in a metropolitan hospital. Her group was doing good work, but Cynthia wanted some extra horsepower from them. I suggested she have a group meeting, and instead of dwelling on problems at that meeting, as they usually did, they should concentrate on successes. This occurred at the end of a year, so it was a natural step for the group to think about the previous year's accomplishments.

The nursing group made a list of things that had gone well that year and that they were proud of. Cynthia then had this information printed on a large sheet of paper, framed it, and hung it in the central nursing station. Not only did her staff start displaying that extra horsepower she was hoping to see, but the atmosphere was more cheerful than it had ever been before. As one of her employees put it, "It's nice to see a reminder that our management pays attention to what we do right, too—not only what we do wrong."

INCREASE ACTION THROUGH BALANCED FEEDBACK

Praise doesn't motivate people. Neither does criticism. What's left? A fair dose of both. Feedback has been called the "Breakfast of Champions." It simply is honest communication about how somebody is doing. Praise, when deserved, should be given. Criticism, when needed, should also be given. People want and need to know the score for their performance to keep on doing a good job or to improve on that job.

To give balanced, honest information to your workers, examine their jobs and work with them to see if there are ways they can find out the score on a regular basis. Arrange for a steady flow of information instead of hit-or-miss, once-in-a-while comments. For example, when employees find out how they're doing once or twice a year in a performance review, or after looking at yearly production reports, the information isn't very useful. To tell Joe in May that you've been upset with him since December because his user-complaint rate is very high doesn't help him very much. He needs to be able to fix the situation when it needs fixing or work out a timely prevention plan. He needs to know there's a problem when the problem is happening, so he can take steps to remedy it right away. In Joe's case, an ongoing complaint/compliment log fixed the problem, so that he can spot trends on a continual basis. Most important, he can see what he is doing well so he won't fix what isn't broken and will repair the areas that are not up to standard.

So often, only the manager or supervisor seeks the production figures, census reports, or other information that gives the overall performance score. To create an action orientation, share this information with your workers on a regular basis. Make sure it's balanced by showing their successes as well as their errors. By having their successes recognized, people strive to repeat them. When you adopt this policy, you reinforce the feeling that you notice when something's done right, not only when it's done wrong, and ultimately you reap the benefits.

THREE WAYS TO PROVIDE FEEDBACK

How do you compile the feedback to ultimately pass on to your staff? Get closer to customers, whether they are another department or division in your company or outside users of your goods and services. Ask their opinions of your services so that you can provide balanced feedback to your staff.

For instance, Stew Leonard's business practices are a favorite topic of many authors who talk about success in business. Tom Peters and Bob Waterman first highlighted Mr. Leonard's Connecticut dairy in their book, *In Search of Excellence*.[1] Most recently, author Ron Zemke talks glowingly about Stew in *The Service Edge: 101 Companies That Profit From Customer Care*.[2]

Mr. Leonard is the owner of a phenomenally successful dairy store. His volume per square foot is ten times the level of full blown grocery stores. He credits this outstanding success to listening to his customers. How does he get close to his customers? He talks to them. You can, too. Stew not only wanders around the store and chats, but he also has Saturday morning conversations with groups of customers. These conversations involve Stew, his staff, and the consumers. He asks, "How're we doing?" They are happy to tell him.

You can do the same thing. Pick up the phone and ask that question.

[1]New York: Harper & Row, 1982.
[2]Ron Zemke with Dick Schaaf (New York: New American Library, 1989).

Arrange for cross-departmental meetings. Wander in, sit down in a customer's office, and ask, "How're we doing? What can we do better to help you?" Then get this information back to your staff. Remember to ask, "What are we doing right?" just in case the customer forgets to mention it. Pass all this on to the people who can do something about it.

A second successful technique that Stew uses is the old-fashioned suggestion box. People are happy to fill it because they know that something will be done about their suggestions, if it is possible. By the way, people do put good comments in suggestion boxes, too.

A third way to find out how you're doing is to create a short questionnaire. Make it focused and easy to answer. For instance, Max, the director of purchasing for a national chemical firm, pinpointed four areas he wanted to know more about. His emphasis was on how well satisfied the users were of the purchasing services in the company: (1) turnaround time for purchase order numbers, (2) availability of the purchasing staff when questions arose, (3) purchasing's capability of tracking past p.o. numbers, and (4) satisfaction with the choices purchasing made. Thus, the survey he circulated in the company is shown in Figure 1.

After Max sent this survey to his user groups, he had his staff compile the results. They then could congratulate themselves on what they were doing well and could work together to fix the problems. Morale and efficiency increased in the purchasing area after the custom of regular surveys was instituted. Now Max doesn't make up the questions, his staff does. Finding out how your staff is doing doesn't have to be a cumbersome or complicated process. In fact, the best feedback systems are simple and easy.

CHECK YOUR COMPLIMENT LEVEL

To increase self-esteem, give your employees recognition through compliments. These compliments can reflect something you've witnessed firsthand, or you can pass on the good words others have shared. You may be tempted to skip this section because you know you're supposed to pay compliments and you believe you do already. Most managers feel this way; however, they usually are unpleasantly surprised when they check the level of compliments they actually give out. Studies have shown that managers believe they pass on positive comments much more often than they really do. Before you check your real

Figure 1.   Feedback questionnaire.

Department _____ Date _____ Name _____

To assist the Purchasing Department in improving its service and helping meet your needs, we would appreciate your assistance. Please fill out this questionnaire and return it to our office by May 15. Thank you for your help. If you have any questions, please call Molly Hearns at x887.

1. When you need a purchase order number, turnaround time from request to answer is:

5	4	3	2	1
terrific		okay		awful

Comments: _____

_____

2. What is the average time you have experienced in getting a purchase order number?

_____ hours _____ days _____ minutes

Comments: _____

_____

3. If you have questions about a purchase order, how available is our staff to answer your questions?

5	4	3	2	1
always there		sometimes		never available

Comments: _____

_____

4. Your ability to track a purchase order number through our office is:

5	4	3	2	1
wonderful		acceptable		awful

Comments: _____

_____

5. What is your satisfaction level with our selections?

5	4	3	2	1
always what I need		medium		you never meet my needs

Comments: _____

_____

compliment quotient, estimate how often you believe you share these positive thoughts with your employees. Then when you complete your tracking, compare your estimate with the actual. Pat yourself on the back if it's close, problem-solve if it's not.

Try the "penny method" to see how well you actually perform. Put ten pennies in one pocket, and each time you pay a compliment to one of your employees, transfer one penny to the other pocket. This is not an accurate measure if you do it only for a day; keep up this practice for at least a week and see what happens. It's a good bet that the first day all the pennies will be transferred by noon. However, by the end of the week, when you will have slipped back into a more normal routine, you may wonder what all those pennies are doing there, still in the first pocket.

A second way to monitor yourself is to use an inexpensive plastic golf score counter. Just tuck it in your pocket, and each time you pass on a compliment, chalk it up on the counter. At the end of a week, check out how well the total matches your estimate.

PEOPLE FIND IT HARD TO ACCEPT COMPLIMENTS

It's surprising and discouraging, when you are making an effort to share compliments, to find out that your compliments are often as difficult for your employees to accept as your criticism. When people are given a compliment, sometimes they respond by trying to convince you you are wrong. When Tim, an office manager for an accounting firm, decided to increase the positive recognition he gave to his staff, he became confused and disgruntled. When he told Alice what a fine job she had done on a special report, her response was, "Oh, don't be silly. Anyone could have done it. It was nothing."

Over and over, Tim encountered this type of response on a regular basis. Unfortunately, the staff's behavior is not unusual. Discounting a compliment is the most common way of responding. How come? From the time we all were tiny folks, we have been taught that to agree with something nice someone said about us is "impolite." We have been taught that the "polite" way to acknowledge praise is to convince givers of compliments that they displayed extremely poor judgment in offering kind words. Sadly, in their good intention of being "polite" or "modest," employees make it really tough for a manager to increase positive feedback. After a while even the most stalwart, persevering manager will give up. Happily, there's good news. You can turn the situation around with these six ways to get your compliments accepted:

1. *Be specific, name the benefit.* Make it as easy as possible for your employees to hear what you are saying. To have compliments register, make them as specific as you can. Just as when you problem-solve, you need to pinpoint a specific job or accomplishment.

Be specific about what it was that they did well, and share the benefit of their action with them. For example, "Jim, when Mrs. Knickers was being so rude at the counter yesterday, you continued to smile and use good problem-solving techniques with her. You even thanked her for bringing the complaint to your attention. I want to compliment you. You handled the situation very well, and that makes us look like top-notch performers." By this simple statement, you reinforce the action that you liked. The employee will be prone to repeat it, you build self-confidence, and you increase an action orientation for the future.

2. *Make it quick.* To get your compliments heard and accepted, say your piece and get out fast. "Getting out fast" can be physically leaving

or simply not dwelling on your comment. Since people feel embarrassed when they receive a compliment, make yours swift and painless. Give them the two seconds it takes to say, "Thank you," then pause and move along with your discussion or your travels.

This principle was played out best by one of my clients' managers. Sally was approached by her boss, who said, "I'm going to pay you an extravagant compliment that I'm fairly sure will embarrass you. So, as soon as I say what I want to say, I'm leaving. You don't need to respond." He then proceeded to do precisely that. Sally's boss told her what a wonderful job she had done on a very important project, turned on his managerial heel, left the room, and shut the door. Sally said that was the best compliment she had ever got because she didn't have to go through the rigmarole of responding "correctly." In addition, she had privacy to savor her boss's words without feeling flustered or foolish.

3. *Cut 'em off.* What if employees insist on talking you out of the compliment? For instance, suppose you say to a staff member, "I appreciated the job you did for Mr. Perkins. It was very thorough and really increased our credibility with him." His response starts out with, "Oh, it was really nothing. Anyone. . . ." Interrupt right then and say, "Don't try to talk me out of it; just say thank-you." Then pick up the conversation from there. All of this, of course, is done with a smile. Your employees will soon learn that what you really want from them, if anything, is a simple thank-you. You'll soon get it.

4. *Be sincere.* Many times, compliments are shrugged off because employees believe they are not sincere. If you rush through an area and toss into the air, "Nice job, folks," the people you intended to compliment aren't really sure what nice job you're referring to. Chances are, they suspect you just read one of those management books that suggest giving employees more compliments.

A gentleman in one of the companies I was working with used to set aside the same fifteen minutes each day to pay his staff compliments. The employees referred to this time as the "compliment cruise." Since they could practically set their watches by this man, they never paid attention to what he said during those times. He believed he was being efficient, but they thought he was being phony.

Generalized, overblown words also damage the credibility of a compliment. "That's absolutely fantastic. Beyond a doubt, the most amazing job in the world," can get old fast. Taking the time to be specific erases most of these mistakes. Employees realize that you have truly paid attention to their activity and the compliments are sincere if you can specify exactly what they did and the benefit that was derived.

5. *Make it personal and individualized.* Some managers believe that they share the necessary positive feedback by using a staff meeting to make a generalized, "Nice job, folks" statement. This, of course, is too broad to be taken seriously.

An additional negative side effect is that the people who worked really hard on a project groan to themselves, "Holy cow. I busted my buttons and a few other things pulling off that job. Tony and Chris did hardly anything and he didn't even notice." In the meantime, Tony and Chris, who didn't contribute their fair share, breathe a sign of relief and go forward assuming that their lack of productivity successfully slipped by you. The end result? People who have contributed so greatly to a project have had their self-esteem dampened, not raised. They surely won't expend as much effort next time, and you're still stuck with Tony and Chris, who figure they can slip by with a low contribution. The remedy? Specifically compliment those who deserve it; problem-solve with those who need it. The staff will stay motivated and productivity will remain high.

6. *Be careful about complimenting in public.* A final caution on compliments. The old adage, "Criticize in private, compliment in public," may not be the sound advice once believed. Staff members have mentioned that, at times, it's difficult to be praised publicly. The other employees occasionally have unusual or difficult reactions. Also, since it's hard enough to receive a compliment privately, the discomfort is only multiplied when people are singled out for public attention.

This is when knowing your team members is crucial. Some people thrive on public accolades while others would rather be buried alive. Some situations are too hot, and you need to be aware of potential reactions to public recognition. Knowing your employees and reading the situation correctly can save you from unintentionally putting some-one at a disadvantage when you simply are trying to pass on some positive words. If you don't feel skilled at reading these situations, ask the opinion of a trusted colleague or your boss. They might be able to help you avert a disaster.

TWO TOP BARRIERS TO ACTION

When people see themselves as capable and competent, they are willing to take action. Each time they experience success, their confidence grows a bit more and they are willing to take even more action. But people don't stick their necks out and try something new or different for two reasons. First, they don't picture themselves as the type of person who takes chances. Second, they are nervous about being able to cope with the results if it turns out badly. To create a can-do team, you must help your staff jump over these two hurdles.

You need to help them focus on the fact that they have already taken many risks in their lives. Most of these risks probably turned out pretty well, too. For those chances that didn't turn out as well as they would have liked, it's a fair bet that these people coped with the situations successfully. In fact, what might have been labeled a failure could even be named a success, based on their way of pulling out of the fire.

Help Members of Your Staff See Themselves as People of Action

To increase your employees' view of themselves as people willing to take chances—therefore action—try this simple exercise. Depending on your goal, you can do the exercise with the whole group or with individuals. You will accomplish some positive team building in a group setting if it's a group that is functioning smoothly already, however, if they are prone to competition and criticism more than collaboration, an individual approach is more productive.

Have your staff members list five risks they have each taken in their lives. Keep in mind that risks are decisions people make about the probable results of uncertain events. In other words, when did they jump into action when they couldn't predict the results? Keep in mind that what is considered a risk by one person will be seen as an everyday event by another. Phillipe Petit, the famous high-wire aerialist, doesn't regard dancing across a cable strung between the World Trade Center towers a risk. His version of a risk is making the commitment to live with someone. Therefore, beware of passing judgment on or attempting to define for another person what is a risk and what is not.

All examples are acceptable, because only the individuals who have had to face their private fears and concerns can determine how difficult they were to overcome. The types of things people commonly list are:

1. Returning to school
2. Giving a presentation
3. Asking someone for a date

4. Speaking up to a boss
5. Confronting a coworker
6. Accepting a new job
7. Taking a trip alone
8. Learning to ride a bike
9. Giving a dinner party
10. Trying out for the choir
11. Playing in a tennis tournament
12. Getting a divorce

After they have completed their lists, ask your staff to pick out which chances they consider turned out successfully and which ones could be labeled failures. Encourage your group to do this from their own perspective, not anyone else's. There is the temptation to use another's standards, particularly when that other person was involved in the adventure, too. So, caution them to be true to themselves only. Usually, more of these risks are seen as successes than as failures. Thus you begin to open people's eyes to the fact that they have taken chances many times in their lives. You knock down their first barrier to action. Their confidence level is increased, because they see that the majority of their chances have had successful outcomes.

Help Them Identify Their Success and Coping Capabilities

To topple the second action barrier, take the exercise one step further. Have your people identify how they coped with those situations they labeled as failures. Chances are, they coped quite successfully. Sometimes failure can be called success, owing to the way it was resolved.

For example, Ted was giving his first big presentation to the marketing group. He decided to liven it up with a joke or two. Unfortunately, he was so nervous about the presentation that he forgot the punch line of his opening joke. In his embarrassment, he asked if anyone in the audience knew the punch line, and three people hollered it out. They all had a good laugh and it grew into a special "in" joke. Changing the incident to a success helped smooth the way for their working relationship.

BELIEF IN LUCK INTERFERES
WITH ACTION

The part employees believe luck plays in their lives has a sizable impact on their action orientation. People who give luck the credit for their successes are not as action prone as those who believe they cause their own luck and success to happen. Researchers have uncovered that individuals who believe in luck are not highly motivated, are afraid of failing when they try something, and work very hard to avoid situations that test themselves.

If some of the people on your team tend to give fate the credit for the good fortune in their lives, try this tactic to turn the situation around. Ask them to take their list of risks and select three that turned out successfully. Have them pinpoint at least three things they did to bring about each of those successes.

For instance, when Julie explored getting her promotion, she came to see that she wasn't simply "just lucky" or "just happened to be in the right place at the right time." She realized that she had taken on extra duties, that she had done some extra study on her own, and that she had attended some company seminars. She also acknowledged that she had made an effort to become more visible in the organization as well as to let her boss know she was interested in promotional opportunities. In other words, she made her own "luck"; it wasn't simply an accident. Julie wasn't aware of how much she contributed to her advancement until she completed this exercise. It turned her thinking around about who was in control of her life and her "luck."

For the chances pegged as failures, have your employees identify three things they did to influence problem solving so that total disaster didn't set in. For example, Steve had volunteered to do a lot of the staff work for some important visitors from one of their firm's foreign distributorships. His intention was to favorably impress his boss with the knowledge that he could handle high-level interaction well. One of his jobs was to arrange for the caterer for a luncheon on the first day of the visit. Unfortunately, the caterer had confused the dates, with the result that Steve was left one hour before the appointed luncheon time with no food and with disaster looming. Instead of buckling, Steve started to scramble. He came up with the idea to serve deli food as an introduction to the "typical American lunch." He picked up pastrami sandwiches, cole slaw, pickles, and cream soda. He served the sandwiches in their paper wrappings, the soda in bottles, cole slaw in plastic containers, and pickles dripped with brine; the guests ate with plastic utensils. His result? The visitors said it was the best meal they'd had since they'd arrived. Eating so casually broke down some barriers and started building rapport, which was the purpose of the visit. Since that incident, Steve had believed that he was just "lucky" not to have fallen on his face. Obviously, luck had nothing to do with it. Because of Steve's efforts, a potential disaster was turned into a success. Insist that your staff members take credit for their good fortune. Help them become aware that they create their own luck. Their action orientation will most decidedly increase.

HELP THE TEAM SET REACHABLE GOALS

How high your staff members set their sights says a lot about their belief in luck, their attitude toward success, and their orientation to failure. People who set unrealistically high goals usually believe in luck, don't have much hope for success, and have a strong fear of failure. In essence, setting goals that are almost impossible to reach is the same as not setting goals at all. It meets their need to avoid testing their capabilities and efforts. It does not meet your need for creating a can-do team.

Setting unreasonable goals helps employees avoid testing themselves because they can escape responsibility for the results, whether they are successful or not. If activities are successful and the goals are reached, their response is, "Well, you never could expect that to happen again. That was really lucky." Conversely, if they fail to achieve those goals, their answer is, "What did you expect? No one could have done it." Either way, the basic message is, "Don't hold me accountable."

Let's take an example. June is a management engineer whose goal was completion of seven ambitious corporate projects within three months. Of course, she wasn't successful in completing a quality job on any of them. When it came time for her performance review, she grew very defensive and said, "What in heaven's name did you expect? No one could have done that." Since of course she didn't receive a raise, let alone a bonus, based on her performance, she chose to leave the company. The sad part is that she repeated that behavior in another corporation, left there also, and is working on a third failure now.

June sets these lofty, impossible goals because she's afraid of failing if she takes on a reasonable amount of work. To avoid testing herself, she consistently sets herself up to fail. Then, when she fails, she attributes it to bad luck; she absolves herself of all responsibility. This pattern can be changed through effective management.

Prove They Have the Necessary Skills to Succeed

As manager, you need to help employees with this tendency to realize that they create their own luck, good or bad. To start building their success and "good luck" quotient, decide that, for a while, together you will establish the goals with those people. Use delegation tips as you assign work. This way, by the time you approach the employees to discuss their projects, you will have established what you believe can be accomplished.

When you hear your high-fear-of-failure workers trying to put in place unrealistic goals, emphasize that you don't expect that level of achievement with those projects. Insist that they tone down their goals. Next, arrange for their success by helping them plan out the projects. As together you break the job down into manageable chunks, suggest that they begin with a step you know will be successful. Use your tight follow-up procedures to ensure they don't squirm out of the assignment.

As mistakes happen, keep employees involved in the fixing process. As success after success pile up, they will start turning around their perspective on luck and realize it is planning and perspiration that does the job, not the winds of fate. Charles Lindbergh always hated the "Lucky Lindy" tag hung on him by the press. According to Lindbergh, there was no luck involved in his solo flight across the Atlantic. As he explained, "It went just as I'd planned it."

Set the Pattern for More Action

To further encourage your staff to see themselves as an action team, have them identify a risk they would like to take. Then have them write this statement on a 3 × 5 card: "I can ————; after all, I did ————." Ask them to fill in the first blank with the risk they'd like to take and the second with one they've already taken.

As an example, Steve wanted to increase his visibility in the company. He knew that one way to do that was to get more involved in making presentations before groups. That, to him, was a huge risk. So, his card read, "I can make a presentation to Production; after all, I learned to ski."

Recommend that employees repeat this statement to themselves several times during the day. This pushes them to more action because they remind themselves throughout the day that they have taken action in the past that turned out well. They also plant the seed for action, which results in action eventually. This is because people cannot continually tell themselves one thing and do another without feeling stressed. If Steve tells himself he can make the presentation, then backs it up with something his mind registers as a good reason why he can, he eventually will do it.

In summary, giving people positive feedback, getting them to see themselves as risk-takers not dependent on luck, and helping them set manageable goals paves the way for your staff to take action. Once the pattern is set, your job consists mainly of providing them resources, keeping the wolf from the door, and giving feedback.

Chapter 8

Prevent Your Employees From Sabotaging Themselves

People often want to take chances and are willing to change. However, there are ways they subconsciously sabotage themselves. As manager, you can help them avoid this.

HELP MAINTAIN PERSPECTIVE

Commonly, people trip themselves up by concentrating on the negative aspects of a situation. And once they start forming the list of negatives, it's easy to keep adding to the list until the whole situation looks out of control. Sometimes, the difficult pieces loom so large that people believe the problem has no possibility of becoming manageable. This interferes with action because people feel they don't have control anymore.

The snowball effect can work in the opposite direction as well. To help your employees gain their balance and prevent a landslide of negative thoughts, have them write down three positive aspects about a situation even if it seems bleak. For example, when the laboratory equipment that had been ordered by a former manager arrived, it was a pretty tough situation. The lab technicians couldn't do their jobs well because the equipment not only wasn't correct, it was down a lot of the time. This situation led to resentment and a lack of motivation to do any of the work, even the jobs they could accomplish. The new manager, Lee, gathered the staff together and asked each of them to come up with at least three positive aspects of the situation. She told them that she wanted them to do this because she had seen motivation drop and felt they viewed the situation as overwhelming. Grumbling but good sports, they came up with the following points:

1. We're learning to work the equipment in spite of it.
2. We're showing how resourceful we really can be.
3. We've learned what equipment not to buy next time.
4. We've learned what equipment and companies to warn our colleagues about.
5. We're learning how to deal with uncooperative companies.
6. We're learning the system so we can get replacements.
7. This'll come in handy even after the lab is in shape.
8. We're pulling together as a team.

Now, listing the points didn't solve the problem. What the exercise did do was restore some balance to their thinking and give them a feeling of having at least some control. With that feeling of control, more effective planning and problem solving could take place, and did. This laid the foundation for success, since the team saw it could have some control no matter how bad the situation looked.

UNLEASH CREATIVITY

Many times when employees aren't taking action, the reason can be traced to a belief that they don't think their ideas are worth much. People discount their ideas precisely because they are their own ideas, not someone else's. If your employees don't think much of their inspiration, have them pretend someone else came up with it, then have them evaluate it. This was a technique used by Scott in the public relations department of one of the utility companies. Scott needed his people to write press releases, but they didn't feel they had the skills or good ideas for releases. He asked them to write one release, then had them pretend their favorite columnist had written it. They thought a lot more of their piece when viewed with this perspective. They were also asked to copy over, in their own handwriting, something by a writer they admired. It was a real eye-opener. Their estimation of the piece went way down when they saw it written in their own handwriting. This exercise energizes people's opinions about their own ideas.

In another example, Peggy needed her staff members to realize they were more creative than they thought they were. Each time she turned to them for a solution, they stumped themselves by saying they weren't very creative. They'd go with the tried-and-true, not necessarily the best ideas and ways. To break this cycle of thinking, at a staff meeting she separated her people into groups of three. She then asked them to come up with as many ideas as they could for using the object she was going to give them.

Peggy handed a paper clip to one group, a rubber band to another, a cup to another, and a book to yet another. She made one rule: not to dump cold water on the process by judging ideas as they created them. (This has the same effect as pushing down hard on the gas pedal and slamming on the brakes at the same time.) The ideas they came up with were a combination of crazy, boring, creative, stupid, and brilliant. For example, a few of the uses the group with the rubber band thought of were:

1. Shoot paper wads
2. Put around a bunch of flowers
3. Cut off the circulation in someone's finger
4. Hold a bunch of papers together
5. Use as a tightrope for a fly
6. Use as a shoestring
7. Hold a pony tail in place
8. Put on your wrist to remind yourself of something
9. Chew on it
10. Snap someone on the arm with it to wake them up
11. Connect your nose to your chin
12. Play a song on it

After they had finished this exercise, they realized that they really did have a creative streak and the process could be fun, not torture.

Peggy then insisted on this same rule of no judging while these employees worked on more important projects. The judging comes later, and the decision model in Chapter 12 shows a structured way to do this, balancing creative options with sensible choices.

MAKE ACTIONS REVERSIBLE

Do whatever is necessary and feasible to prevent your employees from feeling backed into a corner when taking risks. This will lead to more intelligent risks and outcomes, and your staff will enjoy the process more. As the return on their risk-taking investment rises, so will their action orientation.

Often people frighten themselves away from taking action because they believe that, once they are committed to a course of action, they can't change their minds. Better-quality decisions are made in a shorter time when people believe that their decisions can be reversed. This is a powerful force. Research has shown that a decision believed to be irreversible takes twice as long to make as one that can be changed. That amount of time triples when individuals believe not only that the choice is set in stone but that they will be asked to justify that choice.

Coach your employees to determine which actions are reversible and which are not. Help them to appraise action realistically and guide them to see when they are shooting themselves in the foot. Many times, reversing a decision may take some work, but it is possible. Employee awareness of increased flexibility opens the channels to intelligent chance taking.

Make flexibility part of your practice and reward employees who change their minds based on well-founded information. One concern that holds people back from changing their minds is fear of ridicule from coworkers or punishment from bosses. That fear has cemented many decisions that were not the best, when people didn't want to face the "disgrace" that goes with changing their minds.

Quite often, the facts change after a decision is made. Sometimes the facts change simply *because* the decision was made to move forward on a project. Information that was not available earlier may surface, resources may be withdrawn or added. Any number of actions can occur as soon as a decision is made. Make it clear that as the facts and conditions change and an action no longer looks like a smart move, it's not only acceptable to change their minds, it's mandatory.

HELP THEM SEE MORE OPTIONS

Another way people paralyze themselves in the risk-taking process is by believing that there is only one right choice for a solution. In the majority of cases, there are several correct decisions or courses of action. As employees try to decide, have them identify at least three "best" actions. Researchers working on the Harvard Negotiation Project found out that people cripple themselves during the negotiation process by not believing they have good options. They claim one of the most powerful tools for successful negotiation is an awareness of alternative actions. This grants negotiators power and prevents them from giving away the store when they feel their backs are up against the wall.

When your staff members are stumped by a problem, have them come up with ten ways to solve that problem. The obvious choices appear at the top of the list, but the number 10 forces them to dig a little deeper and come up with solutions that might be more creative and innovative. It encourages them to see themselves as accomplished idea generators.

In a typical example, Deborah was the food manager in a resort dining room. She needed to change the dinner traffic flow in her attractive, but not very roomy area, and she and her staff came up with these options:

1. Buffet on one table
2. Entrees on one table, desserts on another
3. Serve salad, buffet dinner
4. Salad bar, serve entree
5. Salad bar, buffet dinner
6. Seat guests at every other table
7. Two seatings only
8. Limited menu
9. Screen in veranda, add seats there
10. Remove bar, put in tables

Naturally, in any environment some methods may be preferred to others depending on the situation, but there usually are a few options. You can coach your employees to look for those options as they make decisions. Chapter 12, on decision making, provides a simple method for choosing among alternatives, so that the optimal action for reaching a goal is chosen.

PROMOTE A WORRY BREAK

Worry is a popular way of interfering with action. When people worry, they give themselves a false sense of doing something about a situation without ever having to put themselves on the line. Winston Churchill once remarked that, "When I look back on all those worries I remember the story of the old man who said on his deathbed that he had had a lot of trouble in life, most of which never happened."

Since a risk involves doing something new, of course it's uncomfortable. By definition, when people take a risk they can't predict the outcome. Accompanying this is a tendency to worry. Taking this into account, create a worry break. For instance, Celia, who was office manager for an accounting firm, saw that her staff was fretting and simmering over the proposed—but not finalized—change in upper-level management. She arranged for Thursday from 3:00 to 4:00 as a time each week for group worrying. She made the rule that they couldn't worry any other time than during the official worrying time. She advised them that, when they were tempted to worry either at work or on off hours, they discipline themselves and wait to worry until the official time.

The trick of the worry session was that it lasted more than twenty minutes. When people fret and stew for less than twenty minutes, they stay at the level of fretting and stewing. When they spend more than twenty minutes, it turns into a problem-solving session instead. This is exactly what happened with Celia's staff. As they worried out loud about what policy changes would be made, they started seeing some ways they could keep control of things that were important to them. They saw that they had choices and that they could problem solve when the time came.

The time spent talking about concerns cut down on the time spent otherwise worrying. It recouped some of the energy that people had wasted being concerned about the changes. It also just about eliminated the side conversations about the situation which had been cutting into work time and only produced more worry and concern. The staff members realized that they had backing from Celia, and together they could and would work out a plan.

When people start to worry, use the decision model in Chapter 12 to show them how to work through their options. Tell them that there's more than one course of action. Use the information on change in Chapter 6, and have them start using their imaginations to their benefit.

EMPHASIZE THE NEED FOR THE
COMPLETE INFORMATION

People sometimes trip themselves up by the amount of information they gather or don't gather when they start to take action. A natural tendency of people in love with a certain course of action is to close their minds to information that contradicts that option. They may say they're open to information, but you will notice that they only get data from people who support their ideas or who provide them with news that reinforces their preferred position. For these evaders, coach them in the need for a sound information search. Through open questioning and problem solving, lead them to see how not searching for information will be to their detriment.

For example, Dan did public relations work for a firm that made enhancements for personal computers, but he had tunnel vision when he wanted to launch a new product. He had his campaign ready and had gathered the support of several popular and reputable computer magazines. When deciding on launch time for the advertising, Dan went to the head of sales, who was ready for the juicy return on investment. The other person Dan turned to for advice was Rick, who was head of engineering. Rick was anxious to get the product on the market because he knew it was a breakthrough, and he wanted to make his splash in a big way, soon.

To avert a possible disaster, the president of the company asked Dan a few pointed questions. Dan had not met with the head of manufacturing, nor had he spoken with the head of planning. With careful questioning, the president helped Dan to realize the questionable results if he launched his campaign when he wanted. He asked Dan what he believed would be the potential results if the orders couldn't be filled. Dan, in not speaking with the head of manufacturing, failed to realize that the tooling wasn't completed because of a wait for parts. He recognized after hearing that news that many customers would be frustrated and turned off when they couldn't get this hot new product. The president also asked Dan to think through which method would be more effective: (1) to launch a series of interrelated products to put the place on the map, or (2) to introduce a disconnected set of products through a disjointed PR and advertising campaign?

Dan reluctantly realized that the coordinated approach would be most beneficial in the long run. He had avoided talking with the head of planning because he really didn't want to know that a series of products was being prepared for introduction. Dan was in love with his solutions, and he didn't want to hear anything that would jeopardize them. By thoughtful questioning, the president helped Dan realize the impact of his limited vision.

GET RID OF BLAME

Blaming someone when mistakes happen is a huge temptation. It's a temptation that costs a lot of energy, time, and motivation and it really interferes with action. People like to blame for a couple of reasons. The most obvious is that, if blame for a situation can be dumped on someone else, then the person doing the blaming doesn't have to take responsibility. The second, less obvious reason is that blaming someone else contributes to a feeling of control; if blame can be assigned, then it seems logical that the responsibility and ability to correct the problem can be as well.

The problem of placing blame is that a lot of time is spent trying to figure out who to blame. Then energy is wasted convincing them that they are to blame. A lot of emotion gets thrown in, which costs time, energy, and money.

Smart management breaks the cycle of blame when it begins. How much better to ask the question, "Where do we go from here?" when things go wrong, instead of investing so many resources in such a nonprofitable process. When your employees start to blame someone else, reinforce your position that mistakes not only are acceptable but are encouraged. Let them know you really believe that, if people aren't making mistakes, they're not trying very hard.

This may be a very different approach for your employees, either because a previous manager didn't treat them this way or because this is a new concept for you. If you are consistent, however, eventually they will realize that you mean it and they won't spend their time figuring out who to blame. They'll use their energy trying to figure out how to solve problems.

AVOID BUCK-PASSING

Sometimes, when employees think a risk looks sticky or they get cold feet about taking an action, they consciously or unconsciously try to pass the buck to someone else. This interferes with their action orientation because they get used to dropping the situation in someone else's lap. The result is that they don't feel the sense of completion that leads to action, and their self-confidence doesn't get strengthened.

One popular way to pass the buck is to end up back in the boss's office asking, "What do you think I should do?" When this happens, lots of managers err by taking the risk away from the employee because they often think it's their job to have the answers and they don't want to put their employees on the spot. A more subtle and dangerous reaction is when they feel flattered that the employee has come to them for advice and they love dishing it out. The problem with these reactions is that they get employees off the hook. In addition, the employees aren't going to be as committed to the solution as they would have been if they had been a part of it. They continue to see themselves as inept, or they figure that the best way to weasel out of action and commitment is to bring the problem to you. Rest assured that they won't change their ways without some action from you.

When employees approach you with this attempt at buck-passing, wave aside the temptation to show how clever you are by providing a solution or action plan. Instead, set some goals with them, use the decision model in Chapter 12, and coach them in developing planning skills. Help them become skilled and competent so they won't want to buck-pass anymore. Instead, they'll be excited about the prospect of tackling new situations. This certainly leads to action, because nothing breeds success like success.

Another way to pass the buck, especially when a decision has to be made or action must be taken, is when employees look for an "expert" opinion. This takes the responsibility for action off their shoulders. Instead of doing their own decision making, they take the opinion of another and run with it. The actions they take based on someone else's opinion may not and probably are not the best ones they could take. If you see any of your employees falling into this trap, step in. The corrective strategies are the same as when they try to unload their responsibilities onto you. Coach them in the necessary skills and knowledge that will enable them to feel confident in taking action.

MAKE SURE YOUR EMPLOYEES COMPLETE PROJECTS

To increase your employees' action attitude, insist that they complete their projects. You have influence through your follow-up procedures. For example, Linda, a manager in a furniture manufacturing company, had such tight follow-up procedures that she seemed to be an elephant who never forgets. If an assignment snuck too close to a deadline without any obvious effort, her employees could always count on a gentle—or, at times, not so gentle—reminder. None of her staff members ever assumed they could slide by an assignment. She held them to their commitments. This had a very positive effect on the staff, and they were famous for being an action group that people could count on.

Linda had an action-oriented team because their sense of completion raised their tendency for action. When people complete projects, they build on their feelings of capability. Things left undone or incomplete rob energy from the next job as well. Insist that your staff complete assignments. Help them come to closure on them, either through a note on a report, an acknowledgement in the mail, or a statement summarizing what they have accomplished and the benefit derived. Monthly reports from each staff member are a sound method of recapturing the good, the bad, and the indifferent while bringing things to a close. A sense of completion is another benefit of delegating the whole job whenever you can.

THREE WAYS TO AVOID PROCRASTINATION

Risk-takers trip over themselves as they invent ways to escape taking action. This is creative procrastination and there are ways to handle it. Let's consider three types of procrastination and how to deal with them.

1. *Maybe you'll forget.* Many times, staff members don't get moving on an assignment, in the hope that you will forget you ever made that assignment. It may be boring or look too hard, or they may feel they don't have enough time. The solution is simple. Have a foolproof, watertight follow-up system. It won't take long for your staff to realize that you're not going to forget an assignment or commitment.

2. *They want to do a perfect job.* Often people procrastinate because they seek perfection. Research has shown that 80 percent of the work is accomplished by 20 percent of the effort invested. Coach your employees to realize that doing a perfect job on every assignment is not only unnecessary but wasteful. Help them experiment.

For instance, Pete, a manager at an opinion-research company, decided to do just that with one of his employees. He needed an assignment completed by Maria, who was a champion procrastinator. He explained the 80/20 rule to Maria and asked her to give it a try. For the management report he needed, Pete asked her to zip up her rough draft, read it through once to clean up any glaring errors, and then give it to him. Of course, Pete had to be careful to not interfere with this process by assuming it would be flawed without a 100 percent effort. Pete and Maria both kept open minds and both were pleasantly surprised. The report was not only acceptable but good enough to pass on to the people who needed to see it—without any more work.

Managers and employees are amazed when this works, and no one usually believes it until they try it. Chances are excellent that you won't need the shine that comes from the extra 80 percent of the effort. Very few projects require the extra investment of time, energy, and money to provide the polish that comes from the additional 80 percent effort. Coach your employees in determining which projects require that kind of total effort and which don't. Then they won't waste time and resources giving 100 percent to all projects, but reserve that energy for the ones that require it. The nicest side effect of this technique is that the incidence of procrastination is dramatically reduced. Every job no longer looks monumental in terms of time and effort, and this prompts people to action.

3. *Your standards are too high*. In the same ballpark with investing 100 percent effort in every task is the problem of your own standards being too high. If employees seem to have difficulty getting moving on a project, review the standards. Maybe they don't have to be as lofty to reach the goal. Another aspect of this is that the job can look overwhelming. This is when your coaching in planning is worth $2 million. Help employees break the job into manageable chunks and attach reasonable time frames for completing the parts. When a job is carved down to size, it's not nearly as frightening.

USE IMAGINATION TO PROMOTE ACTION

Studies have shown that people are much more anxious about doing something if they think about it as a danger or a threat. If employees use their imagination to conjure up the worst scenario, they will paralyze themselves as they gear up for action. Conversely, if they use their minds to lay the foundation for success, they will be an action-oriented team that accumulates more successes than failures.

Help your employees increase their comfort with taking risks by using their imagination. If they are like most individuals, they run a disaster movie through their minds when they contemplate a risk. Assist them in turning that energy away from scaring themselves toward helping them accomplish their goals. Encourage them instead to picture themselves doing very well.

For example, Terry was going to make a presentation for his architectural firm. He was very nervous about this, and to help him along, his boss had him picture the event going very well. He encouraged Terry to see himself as being well prepared, with the audience smiling and nodding as he was making the presentation and then with people coming up to congratulate him afterward. In his imagination, Terry experienced that terrific sensation of victory, and this sent the message of expected success to Terry's subconscious. After all, the subconscious is there to do people's bidding; if they send it messages of success, success will be arranged. If messages of failure are sent, they can count on their subconscious coming through with difficulties.

This isn't magic, even though at times it seems like it. People like to be able to predict their environment. It has a safe feel if they can count on foretelling certain results. Individuals do some very subtle things to make sure they can make statements like, "I told you that would be awful." How much more fruitful to help your team be able to subtly influence their minds so that they can predict good things and end up saying, "I knew it would go well. I was sure they'd like our plan." Creative use of imagination can make that change.

Coach your employees to provide their subconscious with a double shot for success. First, have them picture things going well and encourage them to see themselves basking in glory. Then, just as they get comfortable with this picture, have them see everything turned upside down. When Terry was preparing for his presentation, his boss had him imagine that the audience suddenly started yawning, the projector bulb on the overhead projector went out, and he dropped all his notes and overhead transparencies. Terry had to stay with this nightmare and watch himself pull it out of the fire. Then his boss asked Terry to see himself coping very effectively with the disaster. Terry, in his imagination, had the audience take a stretch break for five minutes. In that five minutes, Terry replaced the bulb, then put his notes and transparencies back in order. He noticed that the audience was wide awake when they returned from their break.

This exercise gave Terry's subconscious the message that he was capable of taking care of unpleasant emergencies. It had the added benefit of alerting Terry to things that had the potential of going wrong. He then could do a little preventive planning. Terry realized he should take an extra projector bulb along and know how to put it in. He decided to number his notes and transparencies. He also built short breaks into his talk so that his audience wouldn't drift off to sleep after lunch.

By stepping in and helping employees readjust their way of operating when they are taking a risk or action, you not only ensure that the risk taking turns out more successful, but you alert them to potential saboteurs. You help employees experience success, you spend your resources wisely, and you make for a much more savvy action taker next time.

Chapter 9

Settle Conflict So It Stays Settled

Stomachs are knotting, blood pressure is on the rise, hands are beginning to sweat. What's up? Conflict is brewing! Contrary to popular opinion, conflict is not unusual, yet we treat it as if it were an extraordinary happening.

Like the air, conflict is around us all the time. No amount of ignoring it or smoothing it over will make it go away. As a smart manager, you have to learn to manage that conflict, since you and your staff will have conflicts with each other, with people from other departments, and with other groups. Conflict resolution is one of the most useful skills you can possess and pass on to your employees. Smart managers capitalize on conflict instead of running away from it or making it worse.

THE INGREDIENTS OF CONFLICT

What do we get into conflict about? You name it, it can be a source of disagreement. People differ in their opinions of how to accomplish things, which are priorities, what are important values, what constitutes someone else's business, how people should behave, how they should think, what is important information. Conflict arises when we think one way about something and someone else thinks a different way. Let's consider some typical types of conflict.

☐ Sandy, a marketing researcher, receives calls from her children, once in the morning and once when they get home from school, which people in the office believe is excessive. Sandy thinks it's none of their business. This creates a great deal of conflict and tension.

☐ Laurie, an employee relations specialist, was raised in a loud, boisterous, "huggy" environment. Giving a spontaneous hug is her way of expressing delight with another. She considers this part of her ethnic heritage, of which she is quite proud, but she needs to be careful in her professional life because she realizes her spontaneity can cause conflict.

☐ The chief of plant operations in a midsize manufacturing company is very detail oriented. His assistant is not fond of detail, preferring to look at the big picture. This has the potential of being a tremendous source of conflict.

☐ Lauraine, a staff employee, and Peter, her project manager, see the execution of a plan very differently. Without discussing and resolving this difference, there could be a huge problem. This situation can lead to performance problems that could have serious ramifications for both careers. In actuality, it's simply a conflict of perceptions.

☐ Some cultures are very private and people in them consider their personal lives off-limits. In an innocent effort to get to know a fellow worker better, the questions, "Where do you live?" "Are you married?" "What does your spouse do?" could cause discomfort and difficulty. No one means to create conflict; in fact, the goal is just the opposite.

☐ How one physically takes care of oneself is a great area for conflict these days. Do you smoke? Do you inhale someone else's smoke? Do you value exercise? Do you tease someone who does? Do you drink alcohol? Do you speak up about your preferences and try to persuade others to do things your way? That's conflict in the making. These areas of difference don't have to be big. They're certainly not intended to drive anyone else crazy, but they cause conflict anyway.

Since the potential for conflict is so pervasive, why aren't we living in armed camps? Because we've learned to deal with these differences, even value them. Differences can be stimulating and lead to innovation. If every difference were erased, what a boring, noncreative world we'd have! Most of us have a truce with the conflict situations we encounter. There are some, however, that are so important they cannot be ignored: the effect of feeling or acting differently from another is cause of great stress, both physically and emotionally.

A Win/Lose Viewpoint

The words *win* and *lose* come up a lot when anyone talks about conflict. These words turn an everyday event into a contest. Everybody wants to be the winner, and nobody wants to be the loser. We set up contests so that winners look good while losers feel bad about themselves as well as lose respect in the eyes of others.

Looking upon conflict as a contest with a winner and a loser introduces an element of game playing into conflict resolution, and then two problems have to be dealt with instead of one. The first problem is the actual disagreement that led to the conflict. The second is the arm wrestling that goes on in the name of conflict resolution. The two problems may not, and probably don't, have anything to do with each other. Someone may win the contest simply because that person has more power, is a big bully, or can be really slick and persuasive. The resolution of a conflict may be disastrous simply because the urge to win is so great and the person with the worst solution comes out the winner.

Intimidation and Avoidance

Most of us grew up without learning how to deal with conflict in a very helpful way, based on what we saw being done around us. Therefore, we didn't learn ways to make conflict work for us. We are uncomfortable with conflict, and uncertain about how to handle it.

Most people cope with the prospect of conflict in one of two ways. Both are nonproductive. Some people act like bullies. They do this to frighten other people into giving in quickly, thereby avoiding long, drawn-out confrontation. They also are bullies in order to intimidate others so that issues which might lead to future conflict won't be brought up. Other people avoid conflict by ignoring or pretending to ignore it. They assume that if the conflict is ignored, it'll go away. If it goes away, it doesn't need to be dealt with.

A Resource Drain

You pay a high price when you avoid dealing with conflict in a win/win manner. Not dealing openly with differences is a dishonest way of communicating. If a group of individuals is dishonest with each other, trust erodes and productivity dies down. Avoiding productive conflict resolution, with you or each other, can be deadly. Often the biggest price is that the problem doesn't get resolved.

Avoiding conflict resolution is disastrous because the issues stay under the surface, creating stress. People say that something is okay with them when it really isn't. Tension builds. Individuals silently boil and bubble until they explode from the pressure. Then, people say things they don't mean—or maybe do mean but could express in a more diplomatic way. The result? First, your employees learn to not believe each other, which undermines trust. Next, people have a tendency to withdraw from dealing with each other. You may avoid your staff; they may avoid both you and each other. Communication breaks down, and productivity suffers. Small problems that could be nipped in the bud grow to monstrous proportions.

Fallout from avoiding conflict resolution can be heavy. Instead of confronting people on issues that are troublesome, people instead resort to sarcasm, nasty teasing (all in the name of "fun"), backbiting, and backstabbing. A lot of disgruntlement is expressed to others but never to the person directly involved. Managers constantly are burdened by being asked to "fix" problems between staff members.

When people avoid dealing with stressful situations, they can find themselves getting depressed, which robs them and the group of energy. Some people get physically ill. Headaches, backaches, ulcers, and depression all take their toll, and your sick roster grows. When people are sick, the work either doesn't get done, you have to hire someone else to do it, or you burden the rest of your already stressed staff with more work. When the people who have been out drag themselves back to work, they are still sick and don't bring the energy and enthusiasm needed to do the best job.

APPROACHES TO CONFLICT
RESOLUTION

Dealing with conflict profitably does not always involve a major confrontation. In some circumstances, ignoring it or smoothing it over is exactly what's called for. If your staff can't distinguish these situations from those that call for making it an issue, they can create some serious problems.

When to Ignore Conflict

When should you turn your head the other way? Sometimes the issue at stake is really small and not worth any kind of a fight. Other times, you know you're not going to get what you want, no matter how much conflict you're willing to deal with or how persuasive and effective you may be. When emotions run really high, it's wise to provide tone-down time for everyone involved so that a real resolution can be hammered out later.

Sometimes, you need more information before a decision can be made. Avoiding conflict until you have enough information is simply smart. In some instances, it's tempting to butt in where we don't belong, but when an issue is none of your business, stay out of it. Other people might be able to resolve this issue much better than you can; they may have more information, better skills, greater interest. Let them.

Every now and then, conflicts can be smoke screens for issues that are much bigger and more important than the one at hand. It's smart to avoid the superficial issue and get to the heart of the matter.

When to Just Smooth It Over

Sometimes, it's a great idea just to plain give in. Don't even put up a smidgen of a fight. When is this best? When the other person has the skills, facts, and information and you don't. At times, we feel our credibility is at stake if we admit we don't have facts someone else does, so we bluff our way through. Don't do it. You can gain a lot of respect if you give in when it's appropriate.

An issue often is much more important to the other party than it is to you. Why fight over something you're not invested in? A friend's mom used to say, "You only get so many fights in this lifetime. Pick them carefully." Every now and then, circumstances find you or your staff member outmatched and losing, without a shred of hope in sight. Instead of skulking off with your tail between your legs, generate some goodwill and enhance your reputation. Give in first and make it look like a gift.

When to Put Conflict on the Table

The majority of the time, when troublesome situations arise they can't be ignored or smoothed over. What are your choices then? The conflict is there because there is a disagreement. Conflict resolution will settle that disagreement, and conflict management is choosing the best way to do that.

The key to effective conflict management is getting issues out into the open and seeing what can be done to reduce the differences. Conflict can be very constructive. It opens up the important issues which can result in productive problem solving. Issues truly get resolved, instead of brewing. Dealing well with conflict opens up communication, which is the bedrock of a good team, and reduces stress and anxiety in the long run. The way you and your employees approach conflict—whether it be with a subordinate, a peer, the boss, another department head, or the VP—will greatly influence whether situations turn into spitting matches or problem-solving sessions.

COMPROMISE: WIN SOME, LOSE SOME

Historically, people have considered compromise as the way to effectively solve disagreements. It certainly has its place. With compromise, you win a little and lose a little. You find a solution that partly satisfies both parties. It is a middle ground that is acceptable to everyone involved, even though no one gets really excited about it.

Certainly there is a place for compromise in the world of conflict resolution. For instance, a deadline can dictate a specific time frame that doesn't allow for thorough exploration of issues. If a situation is allowed to continue, the damage created by the delay would be very costly, so the solution must be settled quickly with a short-term solution.

Every now and then, some portions of an issue aren't that important, so you give in on those points in exchange for something important. Often, there is a large issue that must be resolved, but there are smaller pieces of the problem along the way that can't wait. Compromise is for short-term solutions in order to get to larger ones or more complex issues.

Compromise has advantages, but it also has a downside. Compromisers walk into conflict situations knowing what they would like but realizing they will have to relinquish something. Unfortunately, this can lead to game playing. As one side pumps up its demands, the other side pumps up its demands as well. Both sides try to figure out what the other side *really* wants and how to disguise what it really wants. Compromise promotes the atmosphere of an armed camp, which interferes with sound problem resolution.

There's also a danger in using compromise as your only conflict management style. Sometimes decisions are reached too quickly and are not thought out as well as they could or should be. If people can compromise quickly, they feel successful, and it isn't until they try to implement the solution that they realize some important aspects may have been skipped or glossed over in the race to reach that compromise. By then it may be too late to do anything about it. This style of conflict management carries seeds of dishonesty. If people put up smoke screens and play games, others will learn not to trust them. Compromise can sow seeds of retaliation as well. If people feel they gave up more than they wanted "this" time, they will even the score next time.

COLLABORATION: EVERYONE WINS

If you can't ignore or smooth over a conflict and if compromise isn't the answer, what is? Collaboration. Working together. True problem solving without the game playing. Collaboration is working together to find solutions that satisfy both parties. It doesn't have the bargaining aspect that is in evidence during compromise. It is a very cooperative way of dealing with conflict. Collaboration aims for meeting goals and underlying concerns. It assumes that everyone's needs might be able to be met, and the goal therefore is to work toward meeting them. In other words, everyone comes out a winner. Collaboration is becoming more and more the respected way to resolve issues.

1. *Decisions made by collaboration gain acceptance and support.* Implementation of a solution is not problematic because there is buy-in from all sides. Sabotage or malicious obedience don't become part of the process. All parties feel they have been heard and their points have

been considered, so even if the solution isn't exactly what was desired, each has a chance to work things through and come to a true agreement.

2. *Solutions reached by collaboration generally are much better than those achieved by other methods.* The process allows for input, which helps groups look at all sides and consider all options.

3. *Collaboration builds relationships between individuals and groups.* In these times that call for more and more cooperation and teamwork, it can provide these invaluable elements. Over the long term, there is much less stress when collaboration is used to resolve conflict. The seedy underbelly of conflict—backbiting, subterfuge, sabotage, and withdrawal—are all flipped over and given the light of day; they have no payoff when differences are dealt with in an open and respectful way. When individuals work in an atmosphere of open communication, their energy level is higher, as are their morale, productivity, and teamwork.

This style is noncombative and self-confident. It involves knowing what you want and asking for it, coupled with a willingness to look at all sides and modify requests. There is, of course, a price to pay. Collaboration requires some time. You don't have to spend hours and hours, but it takes time to hear and consider opposing views. It also calls for consistency and trustworthiness. You must work from the same rulebook today as you did yesterday, and you must not lie. You don't fudge and you don't sabotage.

You may need to persuade people that collaboration is the route to go. If they cut their teeth on any other style, which they probably did, you have to dust off your sales skills and help them understand how they can profit from this approach. However, if you convince the people you deal with, and serve as their model for this type of conflict resolution, you can help them take a giant step toward greater teamwork and success.

BE PREPARED

To boost the chances for successful conflict resolution, you and your employees need to do some preparation. This preparation helps clarify the issues before any confrontation and ensures that the best solution for both parties is reached.

The first thing to keep in mind is that the other party is not the enemy. Both of you should come out satisfied. Constantly remind yourself that the idea is not to "win" but to come out with the best possible solution for everyone.

Calm Down

People often get physically worked up when there is a conflict to be dealt with. This interferes with good conflict resolution during both the preparation stage and the face-to-face meeting. To settle down, do something physical: take a walk, do some jumping jacks, run in place. Do anything that'll make your heart beat faster and get rid of some of the adrenaline coursing through your body. You'll then feel and actually be more in control, which is a critical aspect of positive conflict management.

Sometimes it's difficult to find a spot to work out some of your energy. One manager had a plastic basketball hoop on his office door and foam basketball for just such occasions. He gave his body a little physical workout, and gave his mind a rest at the same time by concentrating on getting the ball through the hoop. When he turned his attention back to the conflict, not only was he physically more relaxed but his mind was sharper, too.

People show their tension in all sorts of interesting places on their bodies. Some people clench their jaws, others stiffen their necks, some put it in their lower backs. The result is always further discomfort and possible headaches. A quick self-administered massage is a pretty good idea. Muscles need to relax, and a massage helps that happen. Another way to help muscles calm down is to give an exaggerated wink with both eyes or indulge in several huge yawns.

Breathing deeply has a very positive physiological effect, too. The two common emotions when discussing conflict are anger and anxiety. The rhythm of breathing that accompanies these emotions is quick paced, which produces shallow breathing, which in effect cuts off your oxygen supply. During times of anxiety and stress, the body needs as much oxygen as possible to deal with all that stress. So try to slow your breathing down and take several deep breaths. This will help you think more clearly and will cut the pattern that is only aggravating the situation.

Look at Both Sides of the Issue

The key to successful collaboration is considering both sides' concerns, issues, fears, and information. This calls for operating in an atmosphere of trust and believing that the best solution comes from sharing these things, not hiding them. Collaboration can encourage greater understanding for all parties involved if the information is listened to and considered seriously.

Define what the problem is. Think about who's concerned and what's involved. Look at the problem from the other person's point of view. Dig up some facts so that you're not working solely from opinion or hearsay. A natural result of preparation is that each person or group generally generates a solution. That solution is what each party perceives as the best way to solve the problem. During the confrontation, however, it's important to not get stuck believing only your solution is the answer. Both parties need to regard both solutions as two of the many options that might bring the issue to satisfactory closure.

For example, Byron had just taken over an area of the research division of a major food manufacturer. The previous manager had left a mess, and Byron was told to clean it up. In fact, he was chosen because he had shown a talent for doing this in other areas of the company. His first move was to sift through the different grants and accounts that were involved. To get a better idea of where the money was going, he told the staff that he had to approve any expenditures applied to a certain account. This was because the expenditures were way out of line, and it was impossible to account for where the money was going. His staff, whose postage was applied to that account, were up in arms— angry that even one stamp for a mailing had to get his approval. They believed this would hold up operations.

Byron called a meeting of the staff. He set the tone immediately when he let them know that his solution was just one option; he was interested in their solutions as well. When they laid out their "demands," he said he believed those were other options, too. He then asked them to work with him to find other options, keeping in mind his goal of keeping close track of the account and their goal of not crippling their work.

Eventually they came to a resolution that was neither of the original solutions. Together they decided that expenditures under $50 were at each staff member's discretion and that Byron could review those expenditures every two weeks. Everyone won because the goals of both sides were met.

Don't Scare Yourself

Many people tend to scare themselves to death as they think about dealing with a conflict. They convince themselves that they are going to get annihilated or at least make an enemy. They're afraid they'll lose, that the problem won't get solved, and that they'll lose face and possibly make the situation worse. If this happens for you or your employees, take that energy and picture success instead of failure. Explore each of those fears and ask yourself a couple of questions. Figure out what the realistic possibility is of that happening, and if it does, is the price too high to pay?

For instance, Carl, the supervisor in a division of a large utility, hesitated to speak to an employee about coming in late and not carrying his fair share of the work load. He was afraid that Tim, the employee, would go back to the rest of the staff and "bad-mouth" him. He was afraid that morale would go down and that the rest of the staff would stop being good employees. When Carl explored and exposed this fear to light, other things became quite clear. First, Tim probably wouldn't go back and say he was in hot water with the boss. Even if he did, with some hope of gathering sympathy or allies, Carl realized that more likely the response of other staff members would be relief. They no longer would have to pick up the ball for Tim and could relax knowing that Carl was strong enough to take care of a situation that was interfering with their work. That was exactly what happened when Carl worked up his courage and problem solved with Tim.

Carl's staff was glad he finally did something about a problem that was having a substantial impact on their work. The employees told Carl that they liked a boss who was willing to deal with people not doing their job. It also helped the employees to know where the boss stood. When a staff member "gets away with something," others are resentful and are tempted to "get away with it" as well. If the person in charge confronts the individual and works toward problem resolution, resentment and temptation disappear while respect grows.

Anxiety and stress can prompt people to not think as clearly as they could, and subsequently they can land in hot water. Explore your conflict-resolution concerns no matter how "silly" or meaningless they might appear. These fears generally are what interfere with taking action or, if you do take action, it's done in a way that only makes the situation worse.

Keep Things in Perspective

When upset about an issue, people tend to exaggerate and make mountains out of molehills. This increases their anxiety and of course makes the problem seem much larger and more difficult. The issue gets clouded and blown out of proportion. When this happens, good problem-solving attempts fly out the window. Instead, measure the facts in the situation. Look at the worst thing that could happen, the best thing, and the result in between.

Let's consider how people can sometimes exaggerate. Sally didn't get a piece of information from Merle, a peer, that she needed for a meeting. As she was working herself up about this, she convinced herself that he "always" forgot to give her critical information and "never" considered the fact that she might need it. (Both of those words—*always* and *never*—will lead the other party in a conflict to discount whatever is said. No one ever does something "always" or "never.") Instead, Sally needed to look at how often it had really happened. Sally was upset because this happened twice while she and Merle had been working on the high-priority project. It hadn't happened before this project and, as Sally gave the matter some thought, she realized that the pressure they were working under could have contributed to Merle's behavior. Instead of blowing up at him, she approached him in a way that opened up his ears to her. She said, "Merle, with all the pressure from this project, you may not realize that you didn't send me information about the project meetings last Wednesday and this Thursday." This approach led to a permanent solution.

PICK THE "RIGHT" PLACE AND TIME

Conflict has enough anxiety and stress attached to it that you don't need the additional stimulus of an audience. Deal with conflict in private whenever possible. If the other party doesn't have this priority, request it. If it means postponing the resolution for a short while, do so. Other people interfere with conflict resolution if they aren't an active part of it.

What's the best time to resolve a conflict? That depends. One rule of thumb is to tackle a problem when it appears. Sometimes, as we've said, this works against good conflict resolution, however. If the parties involved in the conflict are very hot under the collar, that's probably not the best time to deal with the issue. If you or your employee don't have all the facts, it's better to wait until you do. You won't get taken very seriously if you are vague or depend on opinion or hearsay. When an important issue is at stake, wait until you have more information to resolve it.

It often takes some time to work up the courage to face a particular conflict. It's never too late to go back and deal with an issue. It's better to go in prepared, calm and ready for resolution, than to deal with it quickly just to get it over with.

Melanie, for example, did just that when she had a run-in with her boss, Bill. She wanted to attend a conference that was in San Francisco. She gave her request to Bill, who sent back a curt no written on the top of her memo. She stormed into his office and said in a very angry tone, "You let your favorites go anywhere they want to. I have worked so darned hard I deserve to go." Her approach put Bill on the defensive. His response was not sympathetic and Melanie burst into tears. She barged out of his office and both were left with a pretty poor taste in their mouths.

During the courage-building time, turn to trusted colleagues for help in sorting out the situation and use them as guinea pigs to practice what you are going to say. Have them help you think through how the other person might react, then come up with a plan. You or your employee will be much more self-assured and therefore more successful when the conflict is actually dealt with.

For instance, Melanie realized immediately that she had handled the situation very poorly, yet she didn't feel comfortable enough to go back and talk to Bill right away. She asked a colleague, Diane, for her advice. Diane always seemed to get what she wanted even when others thought she didn't "deserve" it. Melanie didn't want to talk to Bill about it again until she had some pointers and had calmed down. Together they worked out a little speech that they thought might work with Bill. Two days later, Melanie built up her courage, and with a good sales pitch under her belt and her emotions under control, she requested a meeting with Bill.

The result? The reason Bill couldn't send Melanie to the conference in San Francisco was that three other members of the corporation were going already, and no more than three people from the company could attend one conference. He hadn't told her that when he turned her down because he had been in a hurry and had assumed she knew; he hadn't realized the impact of that no on her requesting memo. Bill didn't share that piece of information when Melanie invaded his office in such an angry state because her way of approaching him made him angry. What Bill was prepared to do was to send Melanie to an excellent conference in New Orleans, where he knew she'd be the first request. In Melanie's calmed-down state, he made her that offer and she was delighted.

This example shows how you can serve as an invaluable coach for your employees. When they are nervous about dealing with a conflict, have them practice with you until they have the words down pat. Have them repeat and repeat and repeat until they get it right.

WHEN YOU CREATE THE CONFLICT

If you are registering a complaint and, in essence, are the creator of the conflict, you can do it so that it gets heard and the conflict has a good chance for resolution. Speak about specifics. Outline exactly what you see is the problem. Talk about the results of that way of operating.

1. *Focus on the problem, not on the people involved.* Problem behaviors need to be identified. Resolutions call for specifics. How much, how often, who, when? It's critical to identify the problem in these terms so you can present a clear case. The idea behind collaboration is to listen to the other party and to have the other party listen to you. Name calling, loaded words, swearing, lies, generalizations, and vague statements all lead to closed ears. Be very clear in your mind exactly what the problem is, and describe it in specifics.

June, a young clerk in the records division of a large company, is our next example. She had the unfortunate habit of yelling an offensive four-letter word when she was frustrated. It wouldn't have been as much of a problem if she had muttered it quietly, however, volume was the issue. Her manager, Roxanne, was very reluctant to deal with this because she didn't know how to approach her. Roxanne understood her frustrations, and she did sympathize with June. To approach the problem, she said, "June, when you get particularly frustrated, as you did this morning, you say '——' in a very loud voice. This carries down the hall. Since we're a public area, this gives a very poor impression about our organization to outsiders. Insiders are questioning our professionalism. I don't care for the word '——,' but if that's the only one you can use in times of frustration, can you think of a way to remind yourself to say it quietly?"

This is the collaborative approach in action. Roxanne has attempted to find a way to meet the needs of both parties. She needs the volume toned down, while June apparently needs a way to relieve her frustration. Roxanne is not barrelling down with her solution, but instead gives her one option. She is willing to consider the options June can come up with. Approached in this fashion, the problem is clear, the solution is the creation of both parties, and the implementation has a good chance of success.

2. *Focus on the benefits to the other person*. People are willing to listen to your concerns about a situation if they make sense to them. Figure out what the results are of continuing the practices that create the conflict. Find things that have some meaning for them. For example, which of the following statements has a greater chance of being heard and acted upon?

☐ "I'm having a problem with something you do and I'd like you to change because it'll make my life easier."
☐ "There is a problem as a result of something you do, and if you change, your life will get easier."

It's no contest. People are willing to do things that work to their advantage. Do some heavy thinking on what benefits are in store if the conflict gets resolved.

This method is a sure winner when your conflict is with people who have more power than you. They often have no desire to resolve a situation because they don't see the price to be paid for continuing the status quo. They also don't see an advantage to doing it differently. Help them see the price and the benefit.

For instance, Joe, a manager of a research team, had a habit of abdication. He continually delegated all his chores to his staff. While delegation is an excellent management practice, Joe went overboard. The result was that the work load of the researchers was inordinately heavy, while the work load of the manager was quite light. This was because 50 percent of the manager's job was research and the other 50 percent was administration, which he continually handed off to the staff. He liked the status quo; his staff didn't. They wanted him to change his practice.

For their approach, they came up with a good reason for Joe to stop giving away responsibility for the administrative portion of his job. They gave him several choices: (1) they would all start doing the administrative work poorly, which would directly reflect on the manager since no one was aware that he delegated the majority of it; (2) they might all leave; (3) they would go to his boss and request some help with their problem. Three good reasons for Joe to change his behaviors. This approach was much more effective than appealing to him through the logic that their jobs were almost impossible to finish with the additional work.

An example in a more positive vein is the group who wanted perform-ance reviews, but had a manager who never gave them. They really wanted feedback, so they approached their manager. Their appeal was that if the manager would please give performance reviews, his life would be easier. Why? The staff would then know when they were on track and when they weren't. Energies could be directed toward the manager's priorities instead of everyone's guessing what he wanted. It would no longer waste resources. Did the manager do it? Yes, he saw how doing what the staff wanted would benefit him—always an effective tactic.

WHEN YOU'RE ON THE RECEIVING END

Sometimes you aren't the instigator of the conflict. Someone else has raised the issue because he is unhappy with something you or your section is doing. Collaboration guidelines work here too, even if the complaining party doesn't know them.

1. *Help the person be specific about the problem.* After all, you can't seriously consider fixing something if you don't know exactly what's broken. Ask for the person's perceptions of the results of operating that way. You then can make a judgment as to whether it's a priority. Don't get defensive and don't attack back. Ask for his concerns, his goals, his problems with the situation. Get as much information as you can. Ask all the open-ended questions: who, what, why, when, where, how many?

To be sure your communication is clear, restate your perception of what he said. Don't just parrot back the words; let the person know you understand the problem. Then share your goals with him and explain what you were trying to accomplish by doing it your way. Talk about options. Be sure you clearly understand what is meant by each option and, if you have some concerns about that option, voice them.

Let's take an example. Ted, the head of a television production crew, was getting frustrated with his client. The script and how it was to be shot had been approved by everyone involved. As Ted tried to proceed, the head of the training group kept countermanding Ted's orders with the people in the plant who were being used as the actors for this training film. Finally, Dave, the training chief who was doing all the interfering, took Ted aside and said, "This isn't going very well. I'm paying you one heck of a lot of money to get it right and you keep blowing it. One more mistake and you're out of here."

Instead of getting defensive or being surly, Ted used collaborative conflict-resolution techniques. He asked Dave what his specific concerns were: "What exactly is it that isn't going well for you?" After a couple more vague statements, Dave finally said, "We need to feature the people more. You keep focusing on the product. That's not what we're here for." Ted made sure he understood what Dave's concerns were by saying, "Let me make sure I understand correctly. You feel that the attention is focused on the process and the product, and you want to highlight the people more. Is that correct?" When Dave nodded yes, Ted continued. "According to the approved script, the emphasis was to be on how to do things and with what products. Do you have a different goal in mind now?" Dave said, "Well, I gave it some thought as we were flying down here and I thought it could be a good PR piece by emphasizing the people a lot more than the original script. I called a couple of interested parties back at headquarters and they gave me the go-ahead." By calm, nondefensive questioning, Ted got to the root of the problem, which was that the rules had changed.

2. *Try listening*. It's hard to hear criticism. Our usual reaction is to defend ourselves. Instead of getting defensive, try listening; you might learn something. By using the collaborative approach, you'll uncover the problem and what the goals are to resolve it. You don't have to come up with an answer at that very moment. In fact, after both parties have discussed some possible options, take at least a few minutes to think them through carefully, without the pressure of confrontation.

With Ted and Dave, this thinking space helped unearth some potential problems that Dave hadn't considered with his spur-of-the-moment decision. It prompted two more phone calls, and the end result was they were to do the shoot the way it had been originally planned. If Ted hadn't responded to Dave's complaints in a collaborative way, there could have been an expensive mess to clean up.

Questions to ask yourself as you consider differences of opinion are

1. Is the concern a legitimate one?
2. Are the results important?

3. Can I meet their needs and mine as well?
4. What was the context of the complaint?
5. How much will it cost me and will the benefit be worth it?
6. Do you hear this from others?

After you've thought about the answers, get back to the other party. Remember the goal of mutual gain and meeting both parties' needs. In collaboration there's never a winner and a loser; there's always a winner and a winner. One wonderful side effect of collaborative conflict resolution is that people are no longer afraid to voice their concerns. You hear about problems while they are still small and easily fixable. You also gain the reputation and respect that comes from being someone who gets things done and helps his employees get things done. People know you will not be walked all over during a conflict, but neither will you attack them. They want to do business with someone who leaves their self-respect intact. With collaboration you not only leave it intact, you may even enhance it.

3. *Don't get sidetracked.* A hospital physician named Dr. Robins would belittle the nursing staff by calling them names in front of the patients and their families. Both the nurse manager and the staff needed to be prepared to confront him when he did this. They practiced at a staff meeting. Quite soon after that meeting, Dr. Robins started his usual shenanigans by yelling at Annie, "You imbecile. You know I ordered a different medication for Mr. Johnson an hour ago. Hurry up and quit being so lazy, and get to the pharmacy to find out why it isn't here. I wish we could get some decent, professional help around here." This opened up several avenues for potential conflict. Dr. Robins' expectation of the pharmacy wasn't realistic. Annie wasn't lazy; she was a real dynamo, actually. There was plenty of decent, professional help around there. All juicy tidbits to leap on.

At the moment of conflict, however, there was one *big* issue. Dr. Robins was yelling at Annie and calling her names in front of the patient and his family. Unacceptable. Instead of rising to the tempting bait he laid out in front of her, Annie handled the situation beautifully. Her response? "Dr. Robins, you apparently have a problem with how this situation is being handled. Could we please go in private to discuss it?"

In private, Annie called him on his behavior.

Dr. Robins, you called me an imbecile in front of the patient and implied that we are not professional here. With this kind of behavior, the patients might lose trust in us, and they certainly will know we don't work together as a smooth team. I don't want this family and patient to go away and tell their friends that this isn't a place they can trust to get good care. Instead of calling the professionalism and credentials of our group into question in front of patients or visitors, it would be good to come up with a plan to take care of your needs without embarrassing any of us. Let's think of what could be done differently the next time you have some concerns about the help you are getting from the staff.

Annie was using true collaboration. She outlined the problem, stated the goals of both parties, and looked for a way to get those goals met. Dr. Robins: he needs an answer when he is concerned about support; the staff: they shouldn't be subjected to yelling and name calling.

When you try to kick off a conflict-management session, first state specifically what you believe the issue is. You can then say, "What's important to you? This is what's important to me." Another way is to say, "What goals are you trying to reach? My perception of the problem is _____. Is that how you see it?" Or, "How do you feel about? . . . Let's examine the possibilities." "What do you think?" Stay focused on the problem. Don't get sidetracked by your emotions or defenses.

Truly listen to the answers. See what you have in common. Determine what goals both of you are trying to reach. In the case of Dr. Robins and Annie, they both wanted the best patient care. Come up with as many options as you can, and see if any of them help you both to get what you need or want. If there isn't one option that's perfect, can you reshape one of the others or combine two to make the perfect solution? If you can't, remember the key words in collaboration. As a solution is proposed, everyone must answer the question, "Can you live with that?" If the answer is no, it's back to the drawing board until the answer is yes. When you get to yes, you can come up with a plan for achieving it.

4. *What is your body saying?* Remember, 55 percent of communication is nonverbal. People respond to you even before you open your mouth. And after you open your mouth, your actions dictate whether they will believe what you say.

Here's some proof of that. Penny needed to confront her manager about something that was very important to her. Her words were assertive, clear, bold, confident, and persuasive, yet her boss didn't pay attention. Why? Because as this young woman made her very lucid statements, she kept straightening her notes and avoiding eye contact with her boss. Her words were perfect, but her actions said, "I'm scared. Don't take me seriously. In fact, don't pay any attention to me. I'm just kidding." And that is exactly what her boss did. Given the option of believing words or actions, most people choose actions. Your actions are the competition you set up when your words say one thing but your body language says something else. Everything must match for you to be taken seriously.

To open the door to productive conflict resolution, your body must convey the message that you are an individual to contend with: you're not a pushover, but you're not a bully, either. You want to show that you are respectful of both yourself and the other person. To do this, stand or sit up straight. Be balanced and relaxed. Hold your head up, straighten your shoulders a bit, plant your feet in a balanced position on the floor.

Make sure your hands appear relaxed. This can mean putting them by your side, in your lap, in your pockets. Just be sure they aren't fidgeting, aren't clenched, aren't jangling pocket change. The main point is that they not be a distraction. If you normally talk with your hands, do that. If you normally don't wave your hands around a lot, don't.

Look the other person in the eye, but break eye contact at comfortable intervals so the other person doesn't feel you're staring. Let that person know you are interested and care what he has to say.

5. *Control your voice.* Apart from actions, the next most important ingredient in presenting yourself during conflict resolution is your voice. A full 38 percent of your message is carried by the way you use your voice. You may have the best words in the world, but they represent only 7 percent of the message. If they come out the wrong way, your whole message can be discounted. For instance, people tend to speak more rapidly than usual when dealing with conflict. Slow the pace down. You'll sound more in control and you'll feel more in control.

To facilitate true conflict resolution and give the impression of confidence and capability, relax your voice. Don't speak too fast or too slow. The tone should be in the middle—not so high that you grate on other people's nerves, not so deadly that you scare them out of their wits. Don't use loaded, offensive words; no blaming, no discounting, no apologizing. Make an honest statement of your position, your needs, your goals. Use objective words and statements. Be direct, don't wander. Don't smile if you don't mean it. Don't nod your head if you don't mean it. Make clear statements in a firm voice with a steady pace and tone.

If this isn't your normal way of dealing with conflict, practice. Practice looking in a mirror, listen to yourself on a tape recorder. Practice until you get it right. Practice with a friend or colleague. Practice, practice, practice. When the lawn fertilizer company, the local photographic studio, or the magazine subscription service interrupts your dinner or your Saturday morning sleep-in, practice. Take advantage of these opportunities to modulate your voice, tone, and pace.

In summary, good preparation paves the way to settle conflicts once and for all. Appropriate words and style of delivery focus on the problem and the issues, not on the people involved. Successful conflict resolution shows a respect for the other person and reflects the goal that both parties come out of the conflict as satisfied as possible with the solution. Both sides get heard. This involves using words that are hearable when delivering a message and working hard to clarify the other person's words when on the receiving end. Resolving conflict in this way keeps it resolved. The issues don't come back to haunt you and drain your resources. The people involved enhance and maintain each other's dignity.

Chapter 10

If You Don't Know Where You're Going, You're Bound to End Up Somewhere Else

This book is devoted to helping you create a team that takes risks, takes action, and gets things done. While fostering this action orientation, you should keep the trite—therefore very true—saying in mind, "If you don't know where you're going, you're bound to end up somewhere else." Identifying goals helps people clarify the exact spot they will end up—which isn't "somewhere else." Establishing a definite goal, therefore, is the first step to getting there.

GIVE THEM A SCORECARD

By setting definite goals, people have a scorecard to record their successes. Nothing encourages further action and success like previous success. When people don't nail down their dreams, they have a vague feeling that they haven't accomplished much that matters. People get so wrapped up in day-to-day responsibilities that they don't take time to notice how they are accomplishing some great things. They don't experience closure or that feeling of having accomplished something big or meaningful. These feelings nibble away at their self-esteem and erode their smart use of energy, time, and money.

Goals that are spelled out keep people enthused and energized. In response to the question, "What if you die?" George Burns, in his nineties, replied, "I can't. I'm booked for the next two years." Goals can keep people excited about work if they're meaningful and challenging. Goal setting can backfire, however, if you as manager decide the goals without input or assistance from the people who have to meet those goals. One of the greatest motivators, after achievement and recognition, is a sense of control over one's own life. By including employees in the goal-setting process, you help them have that sense of control.

Setting goals gives people the sense of control that leads to action. Accomplishing those goals contributes to a feeling of success, which leads to self-confidence, which leads to greater risk taking and even more action. Work with your staff to establish their goals. Check regularly to see how they are coming along. Obviously, some things will happen over which neither you nor your employees have any say. But smart management has you including them in the implementation planning as much as possible. By working together, you can ensure that the work you need done gets done, and that you have employee input and buy-in plus enthusiasm from the start.

QUICK AND EASY WAYS TO
SET GOALS

Instead of having goal-setting sessions that are dull, boring, and tedious, turn them into exciting times that get people enthused. Have your staff nail down what is exciting for them and gives them a feeling of accomplishing something important. Help steer them away from dutifully recording what they think you want or what they're supposed to put down. Once they start experiencing success in relation to their goals, they aren't reluctant anymore. In fact, they get excited.

Many people see the goal-setting process as overwhelming. They tell themselves that they don't have any goals, and that if they did, they wouldn't be very lofty or important. While every goal is not an earthshaker, each contributes an element to accomplishing something that will make a difference. That is really what goals are all about.

To help people overcome these hurdles, capitalize on their main way of learning. In Chapter 2, we discussed the different ways people prefer to process information. Some people do better seeing new things, others do better hearing about new things. Help your people use these preferences to set goals.

Go to the Movies

To start setting goals, have your employees project themselves into the future. Have them pretend that everything is absolutely perfect; it just couldn't be better. Then, for individuals who do better by seeing, suggest that they play a movie in their minds of what is going on in their life at that point. For instance, in October one year, Carol, a dental equipment salesperson, decided to set some goals with her manager. They had just returned from the annual sales meeting in September, so she pictured herself at the next sales meeting on the golf course, doing well. Lots of people were surprised that she could handle a club as well as she did. After the round of golf, she saw herself looking smashing at the awards banquet, where she got inducted into the million-dollar club.

What does this tell us about Carol's goals? During the next year she intends to learn to play golf, because she has realized that it is one of the ways to do business that she hasn't yet taken advantage of. Many of her customers are golf fans, and she gets beaten out on deals by the salespeople who informally interact with those customers during a round of golf. Her receiving the award at the banquet tells us that she has set a 14 percent increase in sales as her goal. On a personal note, Carol realizes she looks so smashing because she has returned to her health club for regular aerobic workouts. It sounds simple and it is. However, in the past Carol was floundering in doubt. She knew vaguely that she wanted to do something different, but wasn't sure what. When she took the time, with her manager's encouragement, to daydream a bit, she was able to pinpoint the actions she wanted to take.

Hearing Is Believing

If individuals are more comfortable processing information through hearing, suggest that they project themselves into that future time.

Once again, they should think of a point in time when everything is terrific, nothing could be better. Then have them pretend that they have just run into an old friend they haven't seen in a long time. They zip off for a cup of coffee or dinner and have a catch-up conversation. Fred, who is chief financial officer for a health maintenance organization, heard himself tell his friend Todd that he was getting known on the circuit as a specialist in the area of risk management. He told Todd he'd given ten speeches across the country in the last year and had been asked to write an article about the topic for a healthcare journal. This helped Fred realize that he wanted to share his ideas with other people in his field, and he wanted to do it through speaking and writing. That enabled Fred to nail down exactly what he wanted to accomplish in the next two years.

Write a Holiday Letter

Another way to pinpoint goals is to have your staff write one of those deadly holiday letters we all get each season. You know the kind.

> *Dear Friends,*
> *We wish you great blessings at this holiday season. We certainly have had our blessings this year. Both kids got full scholarships to Harvard School of Medicine. I got inducted into the $20 million club this year. Alice was elected mayor of New York City, and one of our vacations this year was an around-the-world trip fortunately paid for by the $6 million lottery we won. Spot, our dog, is being featured by a beer company in its ads, and the parakeet won the International Wings Speech Contest. Hope all is well with you, too.*
> *Love,*
> *Chris and Alice*

Have your employees use this type of informational letter to sum up their year's accomplishments. Sam Meyer's letter was a little more modest, but it definitely served his purpose of goal setting; see Figure 2 for his version of a holiday message.

PUT GOALS IN WRITING

When employees write down their goals instead of just talk about them, their accomplishment almost seems like magic. It's as if the goals

Figure 2.   Goal-setting letter.

Dear Everyone:

It's been a terrific year. We revamped the billing process so that we saved the company $22,000. The president herself called to congratulate me. The newsletter finally got off the ground and has been a big hit. I got the training department to sponsor some seminars for my people on customer relations and have already seen the results. I made a presentation to the information group and they have called me for more. This could be the start of the move into their area, which I've had my eye on.

Regards,

Sam Meyer

---

get completed without a struggle or even a lot of purposeful effort. Writing down goals instead of letting them float around in your mind does have this effect, but it's not magic. When individuals write down their goals, it helps subconsciously to focus their activities. The decisions they make as they go throughout their day end up supporting that goal, even if that wasn't the original intention.

Sam, in wanting to implement the newsletter, started subconsciously to make choices that would help bring it about. At the manager's update meeting on compensation, he got an idea for a newsletter article. He started having lunch with different people in the department when they invited him instead of just grabbing something at his desk, as he usually did. Sam did this because he thought he might be able to pick up ideas that could be good for the newsletter. These changes were not made with any great effort, but each action got him closer to accomplishing his goal. They're not results he would have had, however, if he hadn't taken the time to write down his desire and have it permanently tucked in the back of his mind.

After having thought through a goal enough to put it in writing, people subconsciously scan their environment to take advantage of situations as they pop up. They develop the habit of looking for opportunities to get there. And not only do they look for opportunities, but they create them as well.

KEEP GOALS SHORT AND SIMPLE

Make it easy for your employees to put their goals in writing. Million-dollar words don't belong in goal statements. Encourage them to keep the goals simple and short. Goal statements shouldn't be written to impress anyone. They are designed as a road map for accomplishment. Have them write statements that are geared for action and include time frames for completion. Fred, after examining his dream, put together one goal statement: "Present four talks for pay on risk management by January 15." Carol established as her goal: "Play an 18-hole round of golf with a score of 120 or less by August 30." She also wrote: "Compile a list for the boss of ten reasons why my territory should be expanded. Complete by November 10."

None of these statements will make front-page news, but they get the job done. They are clear, concise, and focused. They are single steps to reach the larger goal. And that the way goals are met—one step at a time.

PROBLEM GOAL SETTERS

You may have people on your staff who have tried to set goals in the past and have established some bad habits. Your job is to help them break those habits and establish new formulas that will lead to success. For instance, some individuals are afraid of failing. When they set goals, they often lay before themselves dreams impossible to achieve. With these "impossible dreams" they are rescued from failure because when they don't achieve their goal, they can say, "After all, it was such a long shot, nobody really could have done it." If, by some happy accident, good fortune, or skill, they do achieve their goal, they still discount the achievement, being quick to point out that reaching the goal was a fluke and could never happen again. In other words, they are saying, "Don't hold me accountable for my actions." You, of course, want a team that *is* accountable. Therefore, with these wild goal setters, ride herd on their high-flying ideas and help them bring them down to earth. It will be scary for them, but insist.

Other people who are frightened of failure have a tendency to set very low goals. Once again, they insulate themselves from failure because they virtually assure themselves of success. This doesn't have a very motivating effect, however, because the message they give them-selves is that anyone could have done it and they haven't really achieved anything after all. This attitude serves to keep them from setting meaningful goals that could lead to a sense of achievement and increase their action orientation. They are so afraid of failing that they don't want to take the slightest chance it will happen.

To prime the pump and help them establish higher goals, use the one-step-at-a-time technique. Persuade people to stretch just a little. Keep the stretch to a minimum at first, because when people who are afraid of failing are asked to raise the stakes, they try to boost it up to the "impossible dream" category so they can again avoid worrying about failure. Then keep asking them to stretch a little more, until they start to see the successful results of their effort.

You may also have some employees who have high hopes for success and not much concern about failing. These people tend to set goals in a similar fashion to those who are afraid of failure. They establish goals that either are way out of reach or are so minimal that no one would notice if it got achieved. These people have the point of view that they expect to be successful at whatever they do, but if they aren't, they really don't care much. The key to their goal setting is to make them care. You can do this by encouraging goals that have meaning for them. This is an instance when linking personal goals to work goals has a great payoff. Attach rewards to achieving goals; that has a tendency to make people care if they achieve them or not.

In contrast, people who have confidence in their abilities and believe that they can be successful have a different style of goal setting. These people care about reaching the goals they set and tend to take moderate, calculated risks. Their goals present a challenge, but not such a big challenge that it can't be done without superhuman efforts. By encouraging these people to continue to set reasonable goals and by working toward getting other staff members to set goals in the same way, you ensure a steady stream of successes that matter. You build a sense of pride and accomplishment. All this leads to further successful action.

MATCH THE COMPANY'S GOALS WITH THEIRS

High-productivity teams are made up of individuals who can see the connection between what they are doing at work and their own personal goals. Gone are the days when people worked just for the company. The work force profile has changed and people bring different needs and desires to the workplace. People want to do work that has meaning for them. They want to foster their personal goals through their work. Capitalize on this and turn everyone into a winner, you included.

Stephanie was given a job that her manager deemed "impossible." She was the supervisor of a group whose job it was to produce video-tapes and self-instructional manuals for a technical client. She was informed by her management that it understood that the task couldn't possibly be accomplished in the time frame with the resources at her disposal. A particular problem was the amount of money that was authorized to pay the people who were to develop these materials. The salaries were set at entry levels, yet the work was very sophisticated and called for skilled and talented individuals. Stephanie decided to ignore her management's assessment of the situation.

To everyone's amazement and great delight, Stephanie and her crew brought the project in on time and under budget. At the same time, their work got national recognition for its quality. How did they accomplish this impossible task? Realizing the financial constraints, Stephanie decided not to fight them but to take advantage of them. As she interviewed people for the jobs, she explored their personal goals. The people she picked for her team had needs that could be met by the work she had to do and the training she could provide. They wanted to learn how to develop and produce these programs, and Stephanie was willing to teach them. She inherited some people for the project as well, and she applied the same principle to them. She found out what dreams and hopes were dear to them and made a major attempt to match the work that had to be done with the dreams of these individuals. For example, one of the secretaries wanted to be a writer. When Stephanie found this out, she arranged to have her do some editing of other people's writing. From that step, she became skilled enough to become a writer herself.

By joining Stephanie's team, the rookies learned a craft, were excited about reaching their goals, and worked even harder in spite of the constraints. Stephanie very proudly points out that matching people's personal goals with company goals was the sole reason they produced at such a high level. Not only did Stephanie have a highly motivated work crew, but the word had gotten out that her group was a terrific place to be. Because she helped people reach goals that were important to them, she had a waiting list of excited, enthusiastic people wanting to join her staff.

However you can, try to match your work needs with the personal goals of your employees. That way everybody wins.

IT'S WORTH THE EFFORT

You can encourage all the activity in the world and build a great can-do team, but if that activity isn't focused, a great many of your precious resources—time, money, energy, and motivation—are wasted. Help your staff identify goals and reach for them with every tactic available. Help people chop their goals into bite-size, achievable pieces. Help them figure out what's going to encourage them to reach those goals and what's going to hold them back. Then work with them to reduce the barriers. Problem solve and coach when necessary, and get them through the frustrating times.

Most important of all, help them celebrate when they have accomplished their goals and always give feedback, the "Breakfast of Champions." You'll achieve a great deal with a minimum of waste. In addition, you'll create a very loyal crew, who considers working for you one of the best things that ever happened to them.

Chapter 11

Plan and Organize
for Action

Thomas Edison once said, "I never did anything worth doing by accident."

Plan is not necessarily a four-letter word, but lots of people think it is, for several reasons. Planning sounds scary and complicated. It has a regimented ring to it. People think they can't be creative if there is a plan to follow and feel more comfortable winging it. Planning makes it possible to hold people accountable for activities; this is disturbing for some of us. Planning has an ominous sound and conjures up visions of the War Room at the Pentagon, with flowcharts on the wall and a million lines going in every direction. In spite of all this, planning is a skill you can easily sell to your employees because it can make their lives so much smoother. It is especially easy to convince them if you present the simple model described later in this chapter. But first let's find out why planning is so important.

FOUR REASONS TO PLAN

Planning removes some of the fear and stress from a project. Good planning skills can greatly impact on an employee's willingness to risk and take action. One of the characteristics of successful risk-takers is their ability to plan. This ties in with another characteristic of risk-takers: their lack of belief in luck.

1. *Planning reduces procrastination.* Without a planning model, people tend to procrastinate. Deadlines are not met or are met with poor or uneven work. Projects get handed in, but the work isn't as thorough or complete as it could be. Details fall through the cracks. If there isn't a plan, it's tough to get your hands on information quickly and consistently. Steps are skipped or overlooked, then time is lost running to catch up. The bottom line is that time, money, and energy are all wasted.

2. *Planning reduces stress.* With a planning model, the stress that goes with procrastination is reduced because assignments that normally paralyze people are broken up into manageable chunks. With planning, it's easy to see how the steps of a major project can fit into the rest of the work load. When a project isn't laid out in an orderly way on paper, details that could spell success or failure can get lost. With a planning method, people can stay on top of these details and take care of them, avoiding stress. When a project has a plan, it's easy to find information. You or your employees aren't stuck for an answer when the boss calls or questions are asked in a meeting.

3. *Planning ensures continuity.* As projects are being completed, a plan helps make sure that necessary jobs are taken care of before people move on to the next step. Without planning, so often a group or an individual is ready to move on and can't because something that had to happen, didn't. For example, when Dan was scheduled to input data, he found out one of the codes hadn't been put on it yet. Because his schedule was booked, he couldn't get back to the input process for two weeks. The whole project was delayed because someone hadn't taken care of one simple detail. A plan would have prevented that from happening.

4. *Planning uses resources effectively.* Lots of time, money, and energy get wasted without planning. In Dan's case, he had booked the morning to do the entry. When he couldn't, the project got bogged

down, decisions weren't made when they were supposed to because of lack of critical data, and lots of people were upset. The department looked bad, the manager looked ineffective, and the workers looked— and even worse, felt—incompetent. Lots of time and energy were used up because folks were angry and frustrated.

THREE STEPS TO PLANNING

Practically speaking, the planning process takes tools no more sophisticated than a pencil, an eraser, and a couple pieces of paper. There are three basic steps. First, the tasks that have to be accomplished need to be identified and the resources necessary to pull the job off have to be sorted. Second, the sequence of what has to happen first, second, third, etc., has to be nailed down. Third, a time frame for each of the jobs has to be determined. The following example shows these steps in action.

Justin, an employee in the marketing department of a local bank, was given the assignment by his boss, Marcy, to coordinate a conference for branch managers from three states. Justin panicked because he'd never done anything of this scope before. The job looked huge, and he rapidly felt his confidence slipping away. Marcy saw the writing on the wall and took this opportunity to coach Justin in this planning process. She worked with him to make sure he got the routine under his belt.

Make a List

First, Marcy had Justin think up as many things as he could that would have to happen to pull this project off. She gave him just two minutes, and watched the clock. Here is his list:

1. Purpose of conference	13. Budget
2. Where?	14. Entertainment
3. Who?	15. Fees
4. How many?	16. Registration
5. Speakers	17. Length of sessions
6. Agenda	18. Concurrent?
7. Food	19. Follow-up
8. Refreshments	20. Expo
9. How long?	21. Guests
10. Overnight?	22. Guest program
11. Brochures	23. Youth program
12. Transportation	24. Tickets

Justin's confidence immediately returned when he saw that he was on top of the situation. It's an excellent practice to invest the two minutes it takes to come up with a list like this as soon as a project is assigned. If employees don't, projects can get way out of perspective and the result is that they often paralyze themselves from taking effective action. They keep thinking, "Oh my gosh. I've got a million things to do to get this project done. I don't know how I'll ever pull it off. I don't know where to start."

By creating a list of tasks and resources, employees reduce a project to its real size. The list doesn't have to be complete, typed, or in duplicate. It just needs to get done. By consistently requiring this process from employees, you help them get moving and escape feeling overwhelmed.

Establish an Order

After employees come up with a list, have them figure out roughly what has to happen first, second, third, and so on. In Justin's case, people can't register for the conference unless they know the conference is going to be held, and it can't be held unless there is a spot to hold it. This step is why I recommend using a pencil for this process instead of a pen. It takes a couple of passes before the order is established and the eraser gets a workout.

Justin's list ended up looking like this:

1.	Purpose of conference	4.	Budget
5.	Where?	14.	Entertainment
2.	Who?	8.	Fees
3.	How many?	16.	Registration
13.	Speakers	11.	Length of sessions
10.	Agenda	12.	Concurrent?
19.	Food	24.	Follow-up
20.	Refreshments	15.	Expo
6.	How long?	9.	Guests
7.	Overnight?	21.	Guest program
17.	Brochures	22.	Youth program
18.	Transportation	23.	Tickets

Set Deadlines

After employees figure out a reasonable sequence, ask them to put some deadlines on all the tasks. Remember the old time-management rule that things take longer than they do. So, be sure to include a fudge factor of one-third more time than you think a job is going to take or you want it to take.

To plan a time line is fairly simple. Draw a line with the ending date of the project on the far right and the present date on the far left. Then work backwards from the date you want to complete your goal to the present date. As employees create the time lines, extra jobs and details that may not have appeared at first often show up. For example, Justin listed a brochure as a job to be done. When setting that job on the time line, he realized "brochures" really meant writing the copy, getting it typeset, having an artist lay it out, and sending it to a printer.

One really important thing to remember about this process is that once employees come up with their plans, they aren't set in stone. New information may pop up or a step that should have been included wasn't. Plans that are flexible are the ones that work. The point of taking the ten to fifteen minutes to put a plan together is to put the project in perspective, give it some shape, and assemble a guide for pulling it off.

As soon as a time line is completed, give the employee a folder for the project. Into this folder goes everything that has anything to do with the project, including the planning list and time line. As the employee gathers data, has conversations regarding the project, and completes portions of it, this information gets put into the project file. Then when anyone needs information regarding the project, it's easy to find. The employee doesn't have to check a dozen different places to come up with an answer.

AN EASY WAY TO TEACH THIS MODEL

Teach your employees how to use this planning model, and then insist that they use it for all the projects they take on. This will help everyone stay on top of projects, meet deadlines, and have information at their fingertips. If projects are going to develop glitches, you'll know in plenty of time to head the problem off or work around it successfully.

For example, if one of the speakers Justin wants for the conference isn't available, he has plenty of time to find another that will be appropriate.

A good way to get this model off the ground, and get your employees comfortable using it, is to have your staff try it out during a meeting on a "fun" project. Start by explaining the three steps: listing the tasks, putting them into sequence, and creating a time line. Then turn them loose on a project such as planning a vacation together or plotting a bank robbery. Depending on the size of your staff, you may want to break into groups of two or three.

By trying the model in a nonthreatening situation, they have a chance to play with it and see how it can work for them. It's their opportunity to see that planning need not be cumbersome nor stifle creativity. Giving them the chance to try it out increases the probability that they will use it because they have proved to themselves that it is successful.

Over time, as they use the model more and more, they will get hooked on it. The reduction of stress, which is a natural fallout of using this method, is a nice reward in itself. In addition, your employees will feel—and actually be—in much greater control of their work and their time. Eventually they'll gain a feeling of greater accomplishment. When they know they can be successful at what they try, they will be much more willing to attempt even more. Success with this planning process can lead to heavy action on the part of your employees because the model is simple, easy to use, and brings enormous positive results. Planning provides the game plan for taking intelligent chances and ensuring their success.

GETTING ORGANIZED

Successful action leads to more successful action, so it is critical you help your employees get organized. If accomplishing their goals is a strain, they're not going to be inclined to do very much. Take advantage of the good information on time management on the market today. In addition, here are some suggestions that have been useful for my clients.

Include The Plan in the Routine

Any project, large or small, can be broken into chunks, planned for, and accomplished. To make sure these tasks get accomplished, incorporate the jobs to be done into the regular work plan so that deadlines get met without undue stress or strain. To include these tasks in the day-to-day schedule, you need to put them on a calendar, on a to-do list, or in a tickler file as soon as the deadlines are assigned.

Assign Time Estimates to Each Job

Another way to get a project done is to analyze what has to be accomplished and figure out how much time each job will take. For example, a memo requesting information may take ten minutes to dictate. Analyzing some statistics may take fifteen minutes, writing the draft for a report may take an hour. By classifying the tasks as five-minute, ten-minute, or twenty-minute jobs, your employees use them to fill in time slots that open when they are stuck waiting for a meeting to start, get put on hold, or have fifteen minutes between ending a project and starting their next meeting. The project folder helps this process because everything needed to knock off that fifteen-minute piece is at their fingertips. The fifteen minutes is not wasted looking for necessary details.

Use a Powerful To-Do List

A "to-do" list is exactly that: a list of things that need to get done. There are a few tricks you can encourage your employees to use to make the list a useful tool instead of just a crib sheet.

1. *Set priorities.* Often, people make a to-do list, but don't assign priorities to the items on it. Without priorities, the list isn't a help but, rather, a hindrance, because every time employees look at it, they get overwhelmed with all the things they have to do. The ticket is to decide what's most important, what's second most important, and on down the line. People usually don't like setting priorities because the hardest, biggest, and most frightening job with the largest risk often turns up as the top priority.

Not setting priorities has the same effect as not planning. Some expensive wheel spinning goes into producing a less-than-quality product. By setting priorities, you spend your time the way the smart money spends theirs: where it gets the biggest return. As people tackle these top-priority jobs, the stress that comes with procrastination disappears because their actions are now productive. They begin to accomplish the important items, with the result that they feel and are more in control of their jobs. Once again, nothing breeds greater success and action like initial success and action.

If employees don't have a method for setting priorities, coach them in the *ABC* process. *A* priorities are the most important, biggest-return-on-your-investment jobs. *B* priorities are of medium value, and *C* priorities have low value. Naturally, employees have more items on their list than three, so help them sort through to categorize them all. Assign numbers to jobs within each letter category. For example, Phil, a manager for a large retail chain, had this to-do list:

1. Prepare presentation outline
2. Write costing memo for the boss
3. Write Maniese report
4. Clean Brady file
5. Get printing estimate for brochures
6. Call Sam for P.O.
7. Nail down committee agenda with Linda
8. Copy *Fortune* article
9. Review customer-complaint log

Ray, Phil's boss, helped Phil decide which of the items were very important, which were next in importance, and which were not very important at all. Ray realized that investing this time with Phil initially would have a major payoff. It didn't take Phil long to catch on and start setting priorities on his own. Phil's list ended up looking like this:

A_2. Prepare presentation outline
A_1. Write costing memo for the boss
B_3. Write Maniese report
C_2. Clean Brady file
A_3. Get printing estimate for brochures
B_2. Call Sam for P.O.
B_1. Nail down committee agenda with Linda
C_1. Copy *Fortune* article
B_4. Review customer-complaint log

Finally, encourage your employees to tackle the As, not the Cs. It's very tempting to pick away at the C priorities because usually they are little jobs that can be knocked off quickly and don't entail much risk or stress. Unfortunately, although this gives the feeling of having been busy all day and the opportunity to cross a lot of items off the list, in essence not much of importance has been accomplished.

2. *Review the list on a regular basis.* Suggest that your employees get in the habit of checking their lists every day at the same time. Lots of people do it along with their morning cup of coffee or tea. Others prefer checking it just before heading out of the office for the day; that way, if anything needed for the next day isn't ready, there's still time to take care of it.

A calendar can be a lifesaver when used in conjunction with a to-do list. Have your employees mark on their calendars the things that have to happen to accomplish the goals they've set. Time is just like luck: you don't find it—you make it. Have them make appointments with themselves; for example, have them honor a commitment to write that certain report on Tuesday at 10:00 A.M., just as faithfully as they would an appointment with you. This unbeatable combination of a to-do list and a calendar makes goals achievable. By obtaining tasks from their to-do list, such as a special report, and creating time on their calendar to accomplish those tasks, your employees pick away at projects bit by bit, and lo and behold, two weeks later there is a well-done report ready by the deadline.

3. *Add a tracking column.* By adding a "pending" column to the to-do list, it becomes an even more valuable tool. The column is a tracking list. You know how easy it is for things to get lost in the shuffle of telephone tag. Telephone tag is when you call B.J. to get a certain piece of information. B.J. is in a meeting and will call you back. You are gone when B.J. calls back. You call back and eventually, after several phone calls, you connect. It is not unusual to forget why you called in the first place or who even started the whole thing. Your employees go through the same thing, but you all can stay on top of these events easily with a tracking section on your list.

Jot down a simple, short note about the date and what is wanted. Then, when the connection finally gets made, you won't wonder what the phone call was about in the first place. Likewise, the person on the receiving end isn't kept waiting while you rifle through the files. The status of projects is available at a quick glance. It's very impressive if people consistently get organized, accurate information quickly when they call your department. This is one way to make sure that happens.

4. *Add a goals column.* An additional column for the to-do list is a spot for goals. It's easy to get immersed in day-to-day happenings and

demands and forget the bigger picture. Commonly, when a gift of time falls into your lap—for instance, when a meeting is cancelled at the last minute—the time is wasted. Instead of taking advantage of that time to work on an A_1 priority, there is a tendency to grab what's at hand or deal with some C-priority item because it's quick and easy.

It's easier to stay on top of goals if they are constantly in sight. Naturally, good planning is a critical part of this process. Coach your employees to use opportunities to meet their goals. For example, when that gift of time arrives, they should grab their project folder and pick a job off the list that fits the time slot that's available. If planning hasn't taken place, they generally think something like, "I only have a half hour and that project will take three days of uninterrupted time." Needless to say, three days of uninterrupted time remains a dream. Therefore, encourage your people to take advantage of those smaller gifts of one hour, fifteen minutes, or five minutes that turn up.

With a goals column on the to-do list, it's easy to select what task can be done in the time available. For example, Phil's to-do list is shown in Figure 3.

Files That Work For You, Not Against You

A good filing system can keep your group on top of projects and paperwork, so that details are taken care of and they quit wasting time, money, and energy. Your staff can control events, instead of events controlling them. Usually, the reason most people don't want to use a filing system is that they're afraid whatever they put into the files is lost forever. Work with your staff to devise a system that makes sure this isn't the case. A filing system doesn't have to be fancy; in fact, the simpler, the better. The only people who have to understand it are the ones who have to use it. Remember the reason for a filing system: to be a safe place for information that is easily retrievable. It is supposed to make people's lives easier, not harder.

Put files in alphabetical order, within easy reach, and clean them out once a year. Create two sections: one for active files, with materials being used on a regular basis, and the other for inactive files, with valuable information but not necessary at the moment.

Files of closed projects should be kept in a convenient spot. When your staff completes a project, ask them to clean out the file by throwing away duplicates. Also, the correspondence needs to be put into some

Figure 3. Recommended to-do list.

Goals	To Do	Pending
Pilot for NJ office	A_2 Prepare	Phil 11/10 WCB:
Customer service	presentation	service date
tape	outline	Ken 11/6,7,8: figures
Proposal for new	A_1 Costing memo—	for costing
delivery system	write for boss	Amelia 11/5: seminar
Presentation for MSI	B_3 Write Maniese	dates
on product	report	Pat has computer
Capital equipment	C_2 Clean Brady file	data, call on 12/1
budget	A_3 Get estimate on	Follow up memo to
	brochure printing	SM, 12/6
	B_2 Call Sam for P.O.	
	B_1 Nail down	
	committee agenda	
	w/L.	
	C_1 Copy *Fortune*	
	article	
	B_4 Review customer	
	complaint log	

order. By saving this information, your group doesn't reinvent the wheel when something similar comes along. In addition, you're not left hanging when someone asks for data from last year's project. By keeping inactive files in a separate spot, you don't clutter up the active files and you have the comfort of knowing the important stuff is saved and quickly retrievable.

Hot files are a great time-saving practice. They contain information on top projects of the moment and others that you want to get your hands on at a moment's notice. Hot files belong in or on a desk, or at least easily within reach even when you are on the telephone. If you have to put the receiver down to get to one of these files, they are too far away. With hot files, you can have your hands on information in a matter of seconds; people aren't tied up as you search for data.

Hang Onto Those Good Ideas

A valuable investment is to give each of your staff members a small spiral notebook. These are a great way to capture good ideas. Encourage them to carry their notebooks in their purses, briefcases, or pockets. That way, when they get tired of reading *People* magazine in the grocery line or a great idea hits when they're on their way from one appointment to another, they can jot it down to develop later.

So often, ideas strike at the most inconvenient times or places. Usually, people scramble to find a piece of paper so the idea doesn't get lost. Well, sometimes the paper is found and sometimes it isn't. Lots of times the idea just gets forgotten because there wasn't any easy way to capture it. Even if the piece of paper is located and the idea written down, those slippery scraps have a habit of getting lost.

With a handy spiral notebook, people don't have to play hide-and-hope-you-find with those slips of paper. They're all in one spot. Remind your staff to transfer those ideas on a regular basis to more appropriate spots, such as their to-do list, calendars, or project folders. This encourages action because good ideas don't get lost and employees as idea generators get a boost.

Grab Control of the Time

Coach your staff members in analyzing their use of time. Employees often are unsuccessful at time management because they underestimate the amount of time each job takes. To help them be a bit more accurate in their time planning, have them make a projected log of the activities they have planned for a day or a week and how long they will take. For example, a manager named Chris drew up a log for Monday that looked like this:

1. Allison's farewell—15 minutes
2. Meet with GB on budget—1 hour
3. Evaluation project data analysis—2 hours
4. Staff meeting—2 hours
5. Return phone calls from Friday—15 minutes
6. Outline proposal—1 hour
7. Locate production group—1 hour
8. Meet with communication chief—30 minutes

In actuality, Allison's farewell took forty-five minutes instead of fifteen because Chris ran into Jim and took advantage of the time to discuss the Wednesday meeting. Meeting with GB on the budget took one hour, fifteen minutes, since he was late because he got stuck at another meeting. The evaluation project data analysis took only an hour instead of the two planned, because Chris ran into a snag in the data and couldn't go any further. The staff meeting took two and a half hours since Sam was late and the Samson project discussion took longer than expected. The Friday phone calls which should have been routine weren't. Julie had a crisis and needed advice on how to handle a sticky situation, so that took forty-five minutes instead of fifteen. Chris worked on the proposal outline for two hours because he really got into it. Locating the production group did take the hour Chris had planned. However, the meeting with the communication chief took one hour, fifteen minutes. Figure 4 shows this in table form.

A tidy eight-hour day doesn't stay tidy. Have your staff keep track of why things went differently from planned. Then they will have some clues as to where the biggest trip-ups come from. For example, the meeting with GB on the budget took fifteen minutes longer than was planned. This happened since GB got stuck in another meeting, not an unusual occurrence. So next time Chris has a meeting, he might find it wise to add an extra fifteen minutes to his calendar so he doesn't scrunch himself or anyone else. A good rule of thumb is to plan on one-third more time that you think you'll need for any activity.

Figure 4. The difference between Chris's planned day and his real day.

	Projected	Real
Allison's farewell	15 minutes	45 minutes
Meet with GB on budget	1 hour	1¼ hours
Evaluation project data analysis	2 hours	1 hour
Staff meeting	2 hours	2½ hours
Return phone calls from Friday	15 minutes	45 minutes
Outline proposal	1 hour	2 hours
Locate production group	1 hour	1 hour
Meet with communication chief	30 minutes	1¼ hours
	8 hours	10½ hours

Planning and organizing skills are two of the greatest gifts you can offer to your staff. Most employees have never had good coaching in decent time management. Too much to do, too little time, and no system add to the stress level of the workplace. Money, time, and emotions are wasted when just a few time-management practices could turn the whole situation around. Good planning and organizing skills increase the self-esteem and action quotient of a team.

Chapter 12

How to Make Quick
Decisions That Work

We make decisions to solve problems or move to something better. Sound decisions are a critical factor in producing an action-oriented team willing to take risks. With solid decisions, the risks that your employees take will be successful, which will lead to more action on their part. Coaching your employees in sound decision-making processes ensures that actions they take and chances they go for will be good ones and gives you the confidence to support their actions.

Most people have never learned a good decision process. Decision making is a skill learned much like other skills. People watch others make decisions and then pick and choose what they think might work. Sometimes this is successful and sometimes it isn't.

FOUR INGREDIENTS FOR SOLID
DECISIONS

Researchers have uncovered four factors for making solid decisions that pave the way for intelligent action. First, goals must be established.

Second, a wide variety of options needs to be explored. Third, the consequences of the decision should be looked at, and fourth, contingency plans should be in place. These guidelines help avoid setbacks and remove that feeling of doubt and second guessing that follow a decision.

Making decisions even under the best conditions is hard sometimes. When you and your staff need to decide under less than ideal conditions, such as too little time, not having complete information, or not having enough resources, it is even more confusing. Coach your employees in good decision making to help them around some of these barriers. It's worth the investment of your time to teach them, because once they get the hang of it, the quality of their decisions will be enhanced. You will have confidence that when they make a decision without input from you, the decision will be one that you can back up. This builds confidence for you and your staff and produces a real sense of pride. Your group will be viewed as a team that makes good decisions.

THE TEN-MINUTE DECISION MODEL

Unfortunately, managers often value action above all. The "ready, fire, aim" method of decision making is often the rule. Those words, "We don't have time to think, we've got to act," have torpedoed more projects than any others. But decision making doesn't have to be a long, involved process. Good decisions are the product of orderly thinking. The common way to make a decision is to be faced with a problem, generate some options to take care of that problem, choose one of the options, then act on it. Unfortunately, this method leaves out the important steps that ensure a decision that can be lived with for a long time. The big, quantitative decision models that have been created are excellent, but they often seem of little use when the boss is breathing down your neck saying, "I need a decision now," and you know you'll have to live with the consequences of that decision for a long time.

I've reduced the big models to a ten-minute process that pushes you to look at a situation in the most thorough way possible and select the best choice of action. This model works whether you have ten minutes to make a decision or six months.

Focus on the Goal, Not on the Problem

Instead of concentrating on a problem, focus attention on the goal. For example, Dennis, head of the art department for a major retail store, needed to hire an artist. Lucy, his regular artist, had been in an accident two weeks before and she was probably not going to return to work for six months. Dennis was in a real bind because the department was in the middle of work on a catalog. In his panic, Dennis had quickly advertised for a replacement for Lucy. He had gotten several promising bites and was ready to hire someone immediately. Miles, Dennis's boss, had asked to talk with him before the final hiring decision was made. Miles had been painfully aware that Dennis's decision making wasn't all it could be, and Miles wanted to see if he could turn the tide.

Miles wanted to redirect Dennis's thinking toward a decision that wasn't just a quick fix, but instead was one they could be pleased with. When they sat down to discuss the situation, Miles asked Dennis to nail down his objectives in this hiring decision. Dennis was still focused on his problem rather than on his goal. He explained that he wanted someone to take care of the backlog from the past two weeks, since Lucy hadn't been around to complete the catalog work. Miles, through some careful questioning, got Dennis to start thinking about his goal instead. He helped Dennis see that what he wanted was, of course, a solution to his problem, but that he didn't want to create more problems in the meantime. Dennis's goal was to hire the best possible person for the job, not just get a warm body on board.

In thinking the situation through for a few minutes, Dennis pegged as his objective finding someone who was skilled at drawing, experienced in the type of work he needed done, and could take initiative on projects and making the contacts without checking every move along the way. Dennis wanted someone who could get along with the clients and coworkers, and also someone who could fit into his budget. In addition, he needed someone with clear, concise communication skills because they had to interact with printing companies, newspapers, suppliers, and buyers. Because the company invested so many resources in producing a high-quality catalog, this person was critical. He also needed someone who could learn the work quickly.

Miles had Dennis take an additional step. He asked which of these standards or hopes were absolutely critical and which would be nice to have but were not essential. Dennis realized that he absolutely had to have an individual who was skilled at line drawing, had excellent communication skills, and fit into his budget. He calculated that experience would be nice, but a quick learner with a pleasant personality would be okay, and that initiative would be nice, but not critical. In short, Dennis had defined his goals and focused on them.

Create Options

The next step in the ten-minute process is to create options. In our example, Miles had Dennis sift through the resumés and portfolios he had received. Dennis had interviewed several people and had notes from those meetings. All in all, Dennis had four people he was seriously considering hiring.

Match the Options With the Goals

The third step in the decision model is to match the options to the goal. In our example, Miles had Dennis list the people he was considering, then prompted him to see how well each could meet his goal. A simple way to get this information into one easy spot for comparison is to make a grid similar to the one shown in Figure 5. List the options you're considering down one side and list the goals you want met across the top.

He then instructed Dennis to fill in the blanks. He told him first to look at the things he considered critical and see if all the candidates filled the bill. It turned out that Susan was a very fine artist with her degree from an excellent school, but her line drawing was not as accomplished as her painting. Dennis had been attracted to her because of her talent, but when he realized he needed to emphasize a different kind of talent, she didn't survive the cut. David had the skills, however

Figure 5. Options vs. goals grid.

Applicant	line drawing	communication skills	within budget	learns quickly	previous experience	uses initiative	pleasant personality
Susan		X	X				
David	X	X					
Barbara	X	X	X				
Sam	X	X	X				

he would stretch Dennis's budget beyond the limit and Miles couldn't pull off that much of an exception; David had to be scratched, too.

Barbara and Sam met all the critical criteria. Both were skilled in line drawing, both were clear communicators, as evidenced in their interviews, and both would fit into Dennis's budget. The final choice would be based on the rest of the criteria, which were not critical but would be nice to find in the new team member.

Barbara had two years' experience working at the local newspaper for their advertising section, so the work was very similar. She had to work on her own a lot during that time and was successful; Dennis was confident she could take initiative. The problem with Barbara was that she had a prickly personality. A spin-off of her prickliness was a lack of openness to other people's ideas, so she didn't grasp things as quickly as she might. Sam had worked with an architectural firm doing landscape rendering for the past three years. He had not done the specific kind of work required for the catalog. He scored high on the initiative scale, and he had a sense of humor in tense situations and was pretty even-tempered. Sam was open to ideas and, in fact, welcomed them.

Miles had Dennis assign a number ranking from 1 to 10 for each category according to how well he believed Barbara and Sam fit each of his goals. His grid ended up looking like the one shown in Figure 6.

Make a Choice

The next part of the decision model is the decision itself. In our example, Miles asked Dennis to pick the candidate he thought best filled the bill. To do this, Dennis looked at the numbers and then considered the most important of the remaining criteria. Experience in this exact type of work was a plus, but an individual who had the

Figure 6. Applicant scores.·

Applicant	line drawing	communication skills	within budget	learns quickly	previous experience	uses initiative	pleasant personality
Barbara	X	X	X	4	10	9	3
Sam	X	X	X	7	3	9	9

1 = lowest   10 = highest   X = meets critical criteria

experience Sam had could translate it quickly. Initiative was high on the list, since Dennis had to do much of the artwork himself in order to meet deadlines. A pleasant personality would be a help because the staff worked in close quarters. Diplomacy was part of a pleasant personality for Dennis because the staff had to work with many temperamental people. He didn't need to add fuel to the fire; quick on the pickup bordered on being critical, since they were falling so far behind. With this quick assessment of the important qualities, Dennis chose Sam for Lucy's replacement.

Troubleshoot the Decision

The final step in the decision model is one people often neglect. Miles had Dennis do one last thing before he phoned Sam with the good news: to take a look at what the possible results of this decision could be. One possibility was that Sam might turn the offer down. Another was that, since Sam had never done this exact type of work, he wouldn't be able to perform. Maybe Sam would leave before Lucy returned because his was only a temporary job. If he got an offer of a permanent job somewhere else, Dennis could be left in the lurch again. Dennis and Miles problem solved around these possibilities.

First, if Sam turned Dennis down, would he hire Barbara? Dennis decided that he wouldn't hire Barbara because of her tendency to irritate people. He realized that personality was a much more important factor than he had originally thought. He had several resumés in the pile that could be possibilities, so he wouldn't be left in the lurch.

If it turned out that Sam couldn't immediately translate his architectural experience into usable work for the catalog, Dennis could easily put together a training plan so that Sam could quickly learn what he needed. Miles was happy to provide Dennis with the answer to his last concern. Dennis's responsibilities were going to grow in the next year. Miles could stretch the budget so that Sam would be put on as a permanent employee when Lucy returned. With those thoughts in place, Dennis made Sam the job offer.

Let's look at the factors of making a decent decision a little more closely.

1. *Focus on the goal, not on the problem*. Focusing on the problem instead of the goals gives people the tendency to narrow their options.

Dennis's problem was that he had a deadline to meet and needed a warm body to fill the empty slot. With this negative focus, he was willing to grab anyone who looked able to do the job. There was the very large possibility that he would create more problems in the long run. Focusing on the problem also lent a feeling of lack of control over the situation.

When the problem is restated as a goal, it opens up more potential solutions. The goal of filling the position with the best qualified person opened up a range of possibilities. Dennis also started to see that he could capitalize on his problem instead of just cope with it. He had an opportunity to add a skilled individual to his staff. He felt more in control of the situation. By setting his goal, he got back on the track leading to where he wanted to end up.

Nailing down the "critical" and the "desired" factors clarifies the goal. Decision making sometimes gets muddied because people fail to differentiate between the two. By deciding what is critical to a good decision, you very quickly narrow the options to the usable ones. For example, when groups try to make decisions, frustrations and arguments often are based on this confusion. If a group decides these points ahead of time, everyone talks the same language and heads in the same direction. Deciding what is critical and what is not probably takes the most time in this process. When faced with a decision, do exactly what Dennis did. Have your people list as many characteristics as they can that will make the goal satisfactory. Then, have them sort these criteria into the two categories of critical and not-so-critical.

2. *Create options*. Generate as many options as possible. Go for quantity, not quality. Quantity is the rule, since it's easier to pare down a big list than to build up an anemic one. You want as many choices as possible so that the two or three best are truly best. In addition, one of the ideas alone may not be viable, but in combination with one or two others, it might be a winner. Wild ideas are preferable to tame ones. It's so much easier to subdue a crazy idea than to try and pump some life into a limp one.

Building on ideas not only is legal but is desired, because one thought triggers another, which leads to yet another. The combination of all these ideas can lead to a creative solution. Passing judgment while ideas are in the fledgling stage guarantees they'll never fly. Squelchers like, "We tried that last year," "We don't have the money," "That's ridiculous," or the low moans that accompany some suggestions douse water on not only the idea but the whole process. People are reluctant to suggest an idea if they anticipate getting shot down. As I mentioned before, this is just like pushing the gas pedal to the floor and slamming on the brakes at the same time. But the beauty of multiple options is that crazy, unusual ideas get aired and can be turned into action because of the next step in the process.

3. *Match the options with the goals*. This checkpoint for judging options ensures that the solution you implement is the one that will get you where you want to go. It's simple, it's quick, and it pares the options down in a structured way. If a group uses this process, arguments about options are severely reduced because they match the criteria with the agreed-upon goals.

First, quickly eliminate options by matching the alternatives with the critical criteria. By definition, every one of the critical factors is exactly that—critical. These are nonnegotiable points. Solutions that don't fit even one of these critical factors are eliminated. After the first run through, see how many of the desired criteria are met by the remaining options.

4. *Make a choice*. Look at your assessment of how the solutions meet the criteria. Sort through and decide which qualities are most important, then make a decision as to which solution looks the best.

One caution: sometimes, what looks best puts a knot in your stomach; if that happens, don't hog-tie yourself to that option. Your intuition is trying to tell you something. Trust it, even if you normally don't put much stock in intuition. Your brain is an enormous computer that has stored more information than you could retrieve in many lifetimes. If your stomach starts to knot or your jaw starts to clench when you choose what looks like the best option, perhaps that computer of yours is trying to tell you to look a little further. Maybe you had an experience a time ago which you've forgotten that is alerting you to potential problems. Maybe you didn't explore the options thoroughly enough. Whatever the reason, you're getting a tap on the shoulder. Pay attention to it. Go back and look again at the data you've generated. Maybe the decision could be better. You may decide to go with your original choice, but at least you'll have given yourself the best chance possible to come up with a sound decision.

5. *Troubleshoot the decision*. Since we're such an action-oriented management society, troubleshooting is often overlooked or dismissed as unnecessary. In actuality, it's one of the most valuable steps in this process. Taking a look at possible results before you act offers several

benefits. First, you can prepare for contingencies that might arise. In Dennis's case, he took care of his concerns. By troubleshooting, Dennis had the opportunity to foresee potential problems.

Sometimes the troubleshooting step shows that the decision that looked best will not work when implemented. Time, money, and energy are saved when a new solution is chosen before damage can be done. When troubleshooting, the decision maker can come to realize that all the necessary information, support, or resources aren't available. This calls for actions to make implementation a success. Troubleshooting gives the decision maker the comfort of knowing all the bases are covered when it's time to take action.

YOU AS COACH

To ensure that employees use this decision model, you need to make it part of your own decision-making process. As you and your staff try to decide on a course of action, put the model into play to give them practice and establish it as the way to make decisions. The beauty of this model is that the decisions that get made are of top quality, with a very high probability for success. Employees boost their confidence in being good decision makers. This gets rid of half-hearted attempts and lukewarm efforts at resolving issues and making decisions. It's a thorough way to look at situations and come up with the best answers.

A NOTE OF CAUTION

When managers involve their employees in the decision-making process, there is one cardinal sin that gets committed on a regular basis: misstating the situation. For example, Paul, the manager of the local public television station, walked into his staff meeting one day and said, "Gang, we have to make a decision." Paul explained that the programming had to be changed and decisions had to be made about cuts and additions. That was a fruitful, energetic meeting. They all contributed their ideas, they discussed the issues, and they really invested themselves in the process. When they were all done, Paul thanked them profusely for their help. Gwen, a production assistant, asked when their decisions would get implemented. Paul's reply was, "Oh, these aren't the final decisions. We have to forward these recommendations on to the Board, and they will make the final decisions." Paul was very puzzled the next time he went to the staff for help in making a decision. They didn't get very excited, didn't contribute much, and overall, acted very lethargic.

What happened? Paul told the staff, "Gang, *we* have to make a decision." In fact, his statement should have been "Gang, I need your input. The Board has to make a decision." Be very clear when you ask people to help with decisions. Outline what their authority really is. Paul probably would have got just as much input from the staff with the second statement. What he wouldn't have got was the staff's feeling of betrayal and manipulation. It's extremely frustrating and de-motivating to believe that a decision that's been sweated over doesn't really matter and that the rug is being pulled out from under you.

By using this decision model and being very clear about the level of participation and the authority you share, you'll get buy-in on a regular basis. When you and your staff make decisions together, you ensure their support of those decisions. When people support a decision, they do their best to implement it. Include your staff members in as many decisions as you can. This guarantees the best plan of action from the people who are responsible for implementation. Your team will establish a very stable reputation as sound decision makers. You will shine as the manager who produced that team.

Chapter 13

The Final Leap
Into Action

Jumping into action takes courage. You have paved the way and your team is anxious to take risks and try out new things. They just need that final push into action. There are a few ways that you can help make that leap an intelligent, well-thought-out move with high probability for success. You also can help keep their momentum at high speed.

USE SOMEONE ELSE AS A MODEL

Employees often have the desire to try something new and take a risk, but they're not sure how to go about it. Suggest that they use someone else as a model. For instance, Anthony was an account representative for a metropolitan health maintenance organization. He wanted to talk to Jerry, a coworker, about a habit Jerry had that bothered him a lot. When the two would be working with a customer, Anthony would start a sentence and get very irritated when Jerry would finish it and take credit for Anthony's ideas. Anthony was as good a team player as you're going to get, but he resented Jerry's taking credit for ideas he had sweated over and perfected. Anthony wasn't quite sure how to approach Jerry on this topic. His boss knew that Marlene had had to handle this situation before and had done a very nice job of squelching Jerry's obnoxious behavior. Anthony's boss suggested that he have a chat with Marlene and find out how she handled it.

You can suggest this type of help even when the situation isn't as specific as Anthony's. If workers need to learn how to handle situations differently or want to learn a new skill or a different area, steer them to someone who does that well. Encourage your employees to pick the brains of these people and find out how best to approach the situation. Have them explore the pitfalls and learn how to ensure success. People are more than willing to help in this way. After all, what's more flattering than to have your advice sought out?

TAKE ONE SMALL STEP

Reluctant risk-takers need to taste success. Once they do, the next risk isn't as difficult. Eventually, they act as if taking risks is the only way to do business. To get these people started, ask for one small step. Open the door just a bit. Research has shown that if you can get them to make the first step, they'll take the next step without too many qualms about 75 percent of the time.

Let's see how an example applies to this advice. Amanda had started a catering business. Fortunately, her services were in demand in a very short time after opening her doors. She needed help and she needed it quickly. Amanda always admired how her friend Kate planned neighborhood parties for the kids' birthdays, welcome-home parties, good-bye parties, and just about any other garden variety party. She had a flair that turned even a mundane gathering into a special event. Amanda wanted to capitalize on Kate's gift. The problem was that, although Kate was somewhat willing to join forces with Amanda and provide a service that was so much in demand, she wasn't confident of her ability to pull it off for paying customers. She reasoned that it was one thing to do it for friends and family, and a very different thing to charge for those talents.

Amanda persuaded Kate to give it a shot by outlining one small initial step. Instead of having Kate take on a local fund-raiser, she asked her to do a special theme party for the Crisis Center. These people couldn't pay much for the service, so Kate thought that if she fouled things up she wouldn't feel as guilty. When Kate's party was a success, she was much more willing to try a bigger job with a larger budget. Gradually she increased the size of the parties she was willing to do. Now she donates her talents to the Crisis Center for fund-raisers twice a year. Kate claims that the check for $25, coupled with their admiration of her first job, launched her very successful partnership with Amanda.

This same research has also shown that taking a small step in one area makes it easier to take risks in other areas as well. For instance, John was asked to coach the softball team that his advertising firm sponsored. He was a bit uncomfortable with this because he hadn't coached for many years, but he decided to take the chance anyway. In mid-season, his boss asked him to try his hand at being an account representative and leave his copywriting job. John told his boss he wouldn't even have considered that kind of a leap if he hadn't taken on the challenge of coaching the team. Why did that make a difference? John's self-confidence had grown. His mind was opened to try something new. He had been nervous about the team's success, but by tackling the job he paved the way for future action. Even though the two risks weren't similar, the first made the second easier. Get your employees involved in new things to build their risk-taking muscles.

ENCOURAGE BRIBERY

Encourage your employees to bribe themselves as a way of getting the courage to take chances. Suggest that they not wait until a huge project is completed before they treat themselves but instead build in several reward stops along the way. Make it part of the work plan to offer rewards. By the way, rewards aren't only for successful completion of a job. Sometimes rewards are simply for having the courage to try something. It may not turn out all that well—probably won't if it's the first time for some events. But the fact that the person took the leap is reason enough to come through with a bribe.

The main caution here is to make sure employees don't gyp themselves when it comes to enjoying the reward. Lots of times, people say it's reward enough that they finished a project. They figure that they don't need to spend the time, money, or calories they had promised themselves. Warn them to not do this. They'll sabotage themselves when they again try a bribe to get themselves into action. As they promise themselves that pair of shoes they've wanted if they get the first draft of the annual report off the ground, their subconscious says, "Oh, no you don't! You're not falling for that again. Last time you promised yourself a hot fudge sundae when you screwed up the courage to talk to Marianne. Did you ever see it? No, you decided you didn't need the calories. How can you believe you'll get that pair of shoes? No dice." Tying a pleasant reward to an uncomfortable action reduces anxiety, and instead your emotions become tied in your mind with the thought that something good will happen. This opens the door for more action.

USE SOMEONE ELSE FOR COURAGE

Sometimes the risk is so high and the fear so great that people become paralyzed. Get them past this problem by helping them see who else will or must benefit from their action, even though it's scary. For example, Joyce had quit her job as a sales rep for a home-care products corporation and was starting her own training and consulting business concentrating on customer relations. Her sales strategy was to visit different stores in the malls and experience how their sales staff treated customers. She would identify one or two changes that could help the store increase its customer relations. She then would ask to see the manager and give her sales pitch.

Making this business a success was so important to her that she found herself paralyzed when the time came to make those calls. She got herself over this hump by using her partner, Lana, for inspiration. Lana was newly divorced and a dear friend. Joyce said that when she felt her courage failing, all she had to do was think of Lana. She then realized she couldn't chicken out, if only for Lana's sake. Joyce reminded herself that she had people counting on her, and this gave her the courage to do what she had to do. After she experienced a few successes, she didn't have to resort to this tactic. But it certainly served her purpose in the beginning.

This is one of the reasons why building a team is important for risk taking. In a team members count on each other and pave the way for each other's action. Sometimes it feels more noble to do something scary for someone else than for yourself. Because a team has this intertwined sense of responsibility, it provides the extra boost some people need to take chances.

ESTIMATE THE COSTS

People are sometimes reluctant to take action because of hidden costs. Possibly, in the past, they have been trapped by taking a small step and Pandora's box sprung open. The person who agrees to sit on a committee until a replacement can be found often ends up as president of that committee. So the result is that when you make a request of some employees, their lips always form the word no.

To change that response to, "Sure, I'll give it a try," help them see exactly what they are getting into. Open-eyed risk taking is much more successful than taking action with blinders on. Choices can be made and resentment is not a by-product. Help them see the limits they can accept. For instance, if asked to sit on a committee until a suitable replacement is found, establish a time limit. Philip will stay with the committee for six months or until a replacement is found, whichever comes first. With well-defined limits, people are more willing to take chances.

There are some tangible costs of taking action. An employee who agrees to present a paper at a national conference will lose some time, sleep perhaps, and possibly money. There are some intangible losses connected with action as well. In this instance, the employee may no longer be treated by his coworkers in the same way, his spouse may resent the extra time the project takes, and he may feel badly that he is not spending as much time with his children as they would like. The end result probably has the gains outweighing the losses, but it's wise to encourage an up-front assessment of these losses when an employee is deciding whether to plunge into action. Confronting the losses that may happen not only makes it possible to determine if the gain is worth the loss, but the employee can consider some ways to cut those losses. For example, our friend presenting at the national conference might reduce his spouse's displeasure by inviting her to the conference too. Time might be reduced by investigating whether the material from the presentation can do double duty to satisfy a need on the job.

People are more willing to take risks if they know as much as possible about what is involved: what are the potential gains and probable losses? When people enter into commitments openly, their chances for success increase dramatically.

CRITICIZE THEIR OWN IDEAS FIRST

A good way to build employee confidence in risk-taking activities is to encourage them to be their own best critics. After employees have taken action and the results are in, have them do a balance sheet for themselves. Ask them to identify what went well and what were the shortcomings. Have them figure out why they made the choices they did, even though they may not have turned out 100 percent. This step is important to reinforce confidence in their decision making.

They undoubtedly made the decisions they did for good reasons. By critiquing the decisions, they examine what information and resources they used and they will have some guidance for the next time. Their capability of taking intelligent action goes way up. Employees learn to keep what works and to dump what doesn't. The best part is that they do it for themselves. They don't have you or someone else lowering the boom. Naturally you'll have comments to make, but always have them criticize their own work first. This encourages them to look at action from a variety of angles, and it sharpens their risk-taking skills for the next time.

BEAT DOWN THE BARRIERS

When people decide to take action, there are factors that push them toward pulling it off and others that push them back. Identifying these factors clears the way to action. It strengthens the traits that lead to accomplishment and removes or diminishes the habits that interfere.

Let's look at another example. Alan, an employee of Ted's, was asked to head the United Way campaign for that section. The United Way is the community's set of pooled resources to support a number of local nonprofit services. The force that pushed Alan toward taking on the responsibility is the prestige it offered. Alan believed in the services the United Way supported. He realized that visibility in the company associated with this positive project would be good. He knew one of the rewards for the top campaigners was dinner with the president at his private club.

The factor working against accepting the position is the time commitment. Many people chose not to contribute because they believed the work place was not an appropriate spot for this type of activity. Others always viewed this responsibility as a pushy political maneuver because it was one of the president's favorite projects.

To move Alan to action, Ted helped him see how to strengthen the positive force and diminish the negative one. He suggested that Alan review the work with past chairs and reinforced that fact that this was an honor. Ted had Alan remind himself how much he supported the services the fund finances. Ted then helped Alan plan out the process so it didn't look so overwhelming. He had Alan talk with successful past chairs to find out how they pulled it off. Together, they not only planned the campaign but figured out ways to cut the time involved.

Ted had Alan identify the individuals who didn't support this activity and figure out what his chances were of changing their minds. Or, if he knew they were set against it, how he would avoid annoying or nagging them. By some careful discussion he helped Alan deal with the people who believed that this position was a political maneuver. Did Alan want to do it as a political move? If so, was this all bad? Or was it smart on his part to take advantage of an opportunity to increase his visibility? Alan decided that the barrier was really a plus, because the president did appreciate people who were willing to invest their time and energy in this project. Besides making a contribution to a cause he really believed in, it was a good step for his career as well.

By encouraging your employees to list the plusses and minuses to action, you help them uncover the full range of information they need to be successful. The motivating forces behind an action are reinforced and the barriers to that action either disappear or are diminished. This leads to success and reduces the energy wasted in worrying, which detracts from the real activity.

People often are ready to take a chance, and they just need that final piece in the puzzle to be successful. Help your employees find that piece. Their self-confidence will grow and you will have a more action-oriented team that takes intelligent risks.

Index